HOLT
SCIENCE &
TECHNOLOGY

Animals

HOLT, RINEHART AND WINSTON

A Harcourt Classroom Education Company

Austin • New York • Orlando • Atlanta • San Francisco • Boston • Dallas • Toronto • London

Staff Credits

Editorial

Robert W. Todd, Executive Editor

Laura Zapanta, Senior Editor

Bill Burnside, Kelly Rizk, David Westerberg, Editors

ANCILLARIES

Jennifer Childers, Senior Editor

Chris Colby, Molly Frohlich, Shari Husain, Kristen McCardel, Sabelyn Pussman, Erin Roberson

COPYEDITING

Dawn Spinozza, Copyediting Supervisor

EDITORIAL SUPPORT STAFF

Jeanne Graham, Mary Helbling Tanu'e White, Doug Rutley

EDITORIAL PERMISSIONS

Cathy Paré, Permissions Manager

Jan Harrington, Permissions Editor

Art, Design, and Photo

BOOK DESIGN

Richard Metzger, Design Director

Marc Cooper, Senior Designer

Sonya Mendeke, Designer

Alicia Sullivan, Designer (ATE),

Cristina Bowerman, Design Associate (ATE)

Eric Rupprath, Designer (Ancillaries)

Holly Whittaker, Traffic Coordinator

IMAGE ACQUISITIONS

Joe London, Director

Elaine Tate, Art Buyer Supervisor

Julie Kelly, Art Buyer

Tim Taylor, Photo Research Supervisor

Stephanie Friedman, Assistant Photo Research

PHOTO STUDIO

Sam Dudgeon, Senior Staff Photographer

Victoria Smith, Photo Specialist

Lauren Eischen, Photo Coordinator

DESIGN NEW MEDIA

Susan Michael, Design Director

Production

Mimi Stockdell, Senior Production Manager

Beth Sample, Senior Production Coordinator

Suzanne Brooks, Sara Carroll-Downs

Media Production

Kim A. Scott, Senior Production Manager

Adriana Bardin-Prestwood, Senior Production Coordinator

New Media

Armin Gutzmer, Director

Jim Bruno, Senior Project Manager

Lydia Doty, Senior Project Manager

Jessica Bega, Project Manager

Cathy Kuhles, Nina Degollado, Technical Assistants

Design Implementation and Production

The Quarasan Group, Inc.

Acknowledgments

Chapter Writers

Katy Z. Allen
*Science Writer and Former
  Biology Teacher*
Wayland, Massachusetts

Linda Ruth Berg, Ph.D.
*Adjunct Professor–Natural
  Sciences*
St. Petersburg Junior College
St. Petersburg, Florida

Jennie Dusheck
Science Writer
Santa Cruz, California

Mark F. Taylor, Ph.D.
Associate Professor of Biology
Baylor University
Waco, Texas

Lab Writers

Diana Scheidle Bartos
Science Consultant and Educator
Diana Scheidle Bartos, L.L.C.
Lakewood, Colorado

Carl Benson
General Science Teacher
Plains High School
Plains, Montana

Charlotte Blassingame
Technology Coordinator
White Station Middle School
Memphis, Tennessee

Marsha Carver
Science Teacher and Dept. Chair
McLean County High School
Calhoun, Kentucky

Kenneth E. Creese
Science Teacher
White Mountain Junior High
  School
Rock Springs, Wyoming

Linda Culp
Science Teacher and Dept. Chair
Thorndale High School
Thorndale, Texas

James Deaver
Science Teacher and Dept. Chair
West Point High School
West Point, Nebraska

Frank McKinney, Ph.D.
Professor of Geology
Appalachian State University
Boone, North Carolina

Alyson Mike
Science Teacher
East Valley Middle School
East Helena, Montana

C. Ford Morishita
Biology Teacher
Clackamas High School
Milwaukie, Oregon

Patricia D. Morrell, Ph.D.
*Assistant Professor, School of
  Education*
University of Portland
Portland, Oregon

Hilary C. Olson, Ph.D.
Research Associate
Institute for Geophysics
The University of Texas
Austin, Texas

James B. Pulley
*Science Editor and Former
  Science Teacher*
Liberty High School
Liberty, Missouri

Denice Lee Sandefur
Science Chairperson
Nucla High School
Nucla, Colorado

Patti Soderberg
Science Writer
The BioQUEST Curriculum
  Consortium
Beloit College
Beloit, Wisconsin

Phillip Vavala
Science Teacher and Dept. Chair
Salesianum School
Wilmington, Delaware

Albert C. Wartski
Biology Teacher
Chapel Hill High School
Chapel Hill, North Carolina

Lynn Marie Wartski
*Science Writer and Former
  Science Teacher*
Hillsborough, North Carolina

Ivora D. Washington
Science Teacher and Dept. Chair
Hyattsville Middle School
Washington, D.C.

Academic Reviewers

Renato J. Aguilera, Ph.D.
Associate Professor
Department of Molecular, Cell,
  and Developmental Biology
University of California
Los Angeles, California

David M. Armstrong, Ph.D.
Professor of Biology
Department of E.P.O. Biology
University of Colorado
Boulder, Colorado

Alissa Arp, Ph.D.
*Director and Professor of
  Environmental Studies*
Romberg Tiburon Center
San Francisco State University
Tiburon, California

Russell M. Brengelman
Professor of Physics
Morehead State University
Morehead, Kentucky

John A. Brockhaus, Ph.D.
*Director of Mapping, Charting,
  and Geodesy Program*
Department of Geography and
  Environmental Engineering
United States Military Academy
West Point, New York

Linda K. Butler, Ph.D.
Lecturer of Biological Sciences
The University of Texas
Austin, Texas

Barry Chernoff, Ph.D.
Associate Curator
Division of Fishes
The Field Museum of Natural
  History
Chicago, Illinois

**Donna Greenwood
  Crenshaw, Ph.D.**
Instructor
Department of Biology
Duke University
Durham, North Carolina

Hugh Crenshaw, Ph.D.
Assistant Professor of Zoology
Duke University
Durham, North Carolina

Joe W. Crim, Ph.D.
Professor of Biology
University of Georgia
Athens, Georgia

Peter Demmin, Ed.D.
*Former Science Teacher and
  Chair*
Amherst Central High School
Amherst, New York

Joseph L. Graves, Jr., Ph.D.
*Associate Professor of
  Evolutionary Biology*
Arizona State University West
Phoenix, Arizona

William B. Guggino, Ph.D.
*Professor of Physiology and
  Pediatrics*
The Johns Hopkins University
  School of Medicine
Baltimore, Maryland

David Haig, Ph.D.
Assistant Professor of Biology
Department of Organismic
  and Evolutionary Biology
Harvard University
Cambridge, Massachusetts

Roy W. Hann, Jr., Ph.D.
Professor of Civil Engineering
Texas A&M University
College Station, Texas

John E. Hoover, Ph.D.
Associate Professor of Biology
Millersville University
Millersville, Pennsylvania

Joan E. N. Hudson, Ph.D.
*Associate Professor of Biological
  Sciences*
Sam Houston State University
Huntsville, Texas

Laurie Jackson-Grusby, Ph.D.
*Research Scientist and Doctoral
  Associate*
Whitehead Institute for
  Biomedical Research
Massachusetts Institute of
  Technology
Cambridge, Massachusetts

George M. Langford, Ph.D.
Professor of Biological Sciences
Dartmouth College
Hanover, New Hampshire

Melanie C. Lewis, Ph.D.
Professor of Biology, Retired
Southwest Texas State
  University
San Marcos, Texas

V. Patteson Lombardi, Ph.D.
*Research Assistant Professor of
  Biology*
Department of Biology
University of Oregon
Eugene, Oregon

Glen Longley, Ph.D.
*Professor of Biology and Director
  of the Edwards Aquifer
  Research Center*
Southwest Texas State
  University
San Marcos, Texas

William F. McComas, Ph.D.
*Director of the Center to
  Advance Science Education*
University of Southern
  California
Los Angeles, California

LaMoine L. Motz, Ph.D.
Coordinator of Science Education
Oakland County Schools
Waterford, Michigan

Nancy Parker, Ph.D.
Associate Professor of Biology
Southern Illinois University
Edwardsville, Illinois

Barron S. Rector, Ph.D.
*Associate Professor and
  Extension Range Specialist*
Texas Agricultural Extension
  Service
Texas A&M University
College Station, Texas

Peter Sheridan, Ph.D.
Professor of Chemistry
Colgate University
Hamilton, New York

Miles R. Silman, Ph.D.
Assistant Professor of Biology
Wake Forest University
Winston-Salem, North
  Carolina

Neil Simister, Ph.D.
Associate Professor of Biology
Department of Life Sciences
Brandeis University
Waltham, Massachusetts

Lee Smith, Ph.D.
Curriculum Writer
MDL Information Systems, Inc.
San Leandro, California

Robert G. Steen, Ph.D.
Manager, Rat Genome Project
Whitehead Institute—Center
  for Genome Research
Massachusetts Institute of
  Technology
Cambridge, Massachusetts

Acknowledgments (cont.)

Martin VanDyke, Ph.D.
Professor of Chemistry, Emeritus
Front Range Community
College
Westminister, Colorado

E. Peter Volpe, Ph.D.
Professor of Medical Genetics
Mercer University School of
Medicine
Macon, Georgia

Harold K. Voris, Ph.D.
Curator and Head
Division of Amphibians and
Reptiles
The Field Museum of Natural
History
Chicago, Illinois

Mollie Walton
Biology Instructor
El Paso Community College
El Paso, Texas

Peter Wetherwax, Ph.D.
Professor of Biology
University of Oregon
Eugene, Oregon

Mary K. Wicksten, Ph.D.
Professor of Biology
Texas A&M University
College Station, Texas

R. Stimson Wilcox, Ph.D.
Associate Professor of Biology
Department of Biological
Sciences
Binghamton University
Binghamton, New York

Conrad M. Zapanta, Ph.D.
Research Engineer
Sulzer Carbomedics, Inc.
Austin, Texas

Safety Reviewer

Jack Gerlovich, Ph.D.
Associate Professor
School of Education
Drake University
Des Moines, Iowa

Teacher Reviewers

Barry L. Bishop
Science Teacher and Dept. Chair
San Rafael Junior High School
Ferron, Utah

Carol A. Bornhorst
Science Teacher and Dept. Chair
Bonita Vista Middle School
Chula Vista, California

Paul Boyle
Science Teacher
Perry Heights Middle School
Evansville, Indiana

Yvonne Brannum
Science Teacher and Dept. Chair
Hine Junior High School
Washington, D.C.

Gladys Cherniak
Science Teacher
St. Paul's Episcopal School
Mobile, Alabama

James Chin
Science Teacher
Frank A. Day Middle School
Newtonville, Massachusetts

Kenneth Creese
Science Teacher
White Mountain Junior High
School
Rock Springs, Wyoming

Linda A. Culp
Science Teacher and Dept. Chair
Thorndale High School
Thorndale, Texas

Georgiann Delgadillo
Science Teacher
East Valley Continuous
Curriculum School
Spokane, Washington

Alonda Droege
Biology Teacher
Evergreen High School
Seattle, Washington

Michael J. DuPré
Curriculum Specialist
Rush Henrietta Junior-Senior
High School
Henrietta, New York

Rebecca Ferguson
Science Teacher
North Ridge Middle School
North Richland Hills, Texas

Susan Gorman
Science Teacher
North Ridge Middle School
North Richland Hills, Texas

Gary Habeeb
Science Mentor
Sierra-Plumas Joint Unified
School District
Downieville, California

Karma Houston-Hughes
Science Mentor
Kyrene Middle School
Tempe, Arizona

Roberta Jacobowitz
Science Teacher
C. W. Otto Middle School
Lansing, Michigan

Kerry A. Johnson
Science Teacher
Isbell Middle School
Santa Paula, California

M. R. Penny Kisiah
Science Teacher and Dept. Chair
Fairview Middle School
Tallahassee, Florida

Kathy LaRoe
Science Teacher
East Valley Middle School
East Helena, Montana

Jane M. Lemons
Science Teacher
Western Rockingham Middle
School
Madison, North Carolina

Scott Mandel, Ph.D.
*Director and Educational
Consultant*
Teachers Helping Teachers
Los Angeles, California

Thomas Manerchia
*Former Biology and Life Science
Teacher*
Archmere Academy
Claymont, Delaware

Maurine O. Marchani
Science Teacher and Dept. Chair
Raymond Park Middle School
Indianapolis, Indiana

Jason P. Marsh
Biology Teacher
Montevideo High School and
Montevideo Country School
Montevideo, Minnesota

Edith C. McAlanis
Science Teacher and Dept. Chair
Socorro Middle School
El Paso, Texas

Kevin McCurdy, Ph.D.
Science Teacher
Elmwood Junior High School
Rogers, Arkansas

Kathy McKee
Science Teacher
Hoyt Middle School
Des Moines, Iowa

Alyson Mike
Science Teacher
East Valley Middle School
East Helena, Montana

Donna Norwood
Science Teacher and Dept. Chair
Monroe Middle School
Charlotte, North Carolina

James B. Pulley
Former Science Teacher
Liberty High School
Liberty, Missouri

Terry J. Rakes
Science Teacher
Elmwood Junior High School
Rogers, Arkansas

Elizabeth Rustad
Science Teacher
Crane Middle School
Yuma, Arizona

Debra A. Sampson
Science Teacher
Booker T. Washington Middle
School
Elgin, Texas

Charles Schindler
Curriculum Advisor
San Bernadino City Unified
Schools
San Bernadino, California

Bert J. Sherwood
Science Teacher
Socorro Middle School
El Paso, Texas

Patricia McFarlane Soto
Science Teacher and Dept. Chair
G. W. Carver Middle School
Miami, Florida

David M. Sparks
Science Teacher
Redwater Junior High School
Redwater, Texas

Elizabeth Truax
Science Teacher
Lewiston-Porter Central
School
Lewiston, New York

Ivora Washington
Science Teacher and Dept. Chair
Hyattsville Middle School
Washington, D.C.

Elsie N. Waynes
Science Teacher and Dept. Chair
R. H. Terrell Junior High
School
Washington, D.C.

Nancy Wesorick
Science and Math Teacher
Sunset Middle School
Longmont, Colorado

Alexis S. Wright
*Middle School Science
Coordinator*
Rye Country Day School
Rye, New York

John Zambo
Science Teacher
E. Ustach Middle School
Modesto, California

Gordon Zibelman
Science Teacher
Drexell Hill Middle School
Drexell Hill, Pennsylvania

Animals

Skills Development

To the Student

This book was created to make your science experience interesting, exciting, and fun!

Go for It!

Science is a process of discovery, a trek into the unknown. The skills you develop using *Holt Science & Technology*— such as observing, experimenting, and explaining observations and ideas— are the skills you will need for the future. There is a universe of exploration and discovery awaiting those who accept the challenges of science.

Science & Technology

You see the interaction between science and technology every day. Science makes technology possible. On the other hand, some of the products of technology, such as computers, are used to make further scientific discoveries. In fact, much of the scientific work that is done today has become so technically complicated and expensive that no one person can do it entirely alone. But make no mistake, the creative ideas for even the most highly technical and expensive scientific work still come from individuals.

Activities and Labs

The activities and labs in this book will allow you to make some basic but important scientific discoveries on your own. You can even do some exploring on your own at home! Here's your chance to use your imagination and curiosity as you investigate your world.

Keep a ScienceLog

In this book, you will be asked to keep a type of journal called a ScienceLog to record your thoughts, observations, experiments, and conclusions. As you develop your ScienceLog, you will see your own ideas taking shape over time. You'll have a written record of how your ideas have changed as you learn about and explore interesting topics in science.

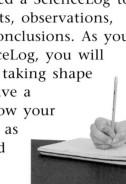

Know "What You'll Do"

The "What You'll Do" list at the beginning of each section is your built-in guide to what you need to learn in each chapter. When you can answer the questions in the Section Review and Chapter Review, you know you are ready for a test.

Check Out the Internet

You will see this $^{SC}_{LINKS}$ logo throughout the book. You'll be using *sci*LINKS as your gateway to the Internet. Once you log on to *sci*LINKS using your computer's Internet link, type in the *sci*LINKS address. When asked for the keyword code, type in the keyword for that topic. A wealth of resources is now at your disposal to help you learn more about that topic.

In addition to *sci*LINKS you can log on to some other great resources to go with your text. The addresses shown below will take you to the home page of each site.

internet**connect**

This textbook contains the following on-line resources to help you make the most of your science experience.

 go. hrw .com

Visit **go.hrw.com** for extra help and study aids matched to your textbook. Just type in the keyword HST HOME.

 SC*i*LINKS **NSTA**

Visit **www.scilinks.org** to find resources specific to topics in your textbook. Keywords appear throughout your book to take you further.

 Smithsonian Institution® **Internet Connections**

Visit **www.si.edu/hrw** for specifically chosen on-line materials from one of our nation's premier science museums.

CNNfyi.com

Visit **www.cnnfyi.com** for late-breaking news and current events stories selected just for you.

Animals and Behavior

Pre-Reading Questions

1. What characteristics make an animal different from a plant?

2. How do animals know when to migrate?

GOTCHA!

This spider needs to eat in order to survive. On the other hand, this bumblebee needs to avoid being eaten. It has to escape in order to survive. How do the spider, the bumblebee, and other animals get what they need in order to live? In this chapter you will learn what it means to be an animal. You will also learn how animals live, reproduce, and behave.

GO ON A SAFARI!

You don't have to travel far to see interesting animals. If you look closely, you are sure to find animals nearby.

Procedure

1. Go outside and find **two different animals** to observe.

2. Without disturbing the animals, sit quietly and watch them for a few minutes from a distance. You may want to use **binoculars** or a **magnifying lens.**

   Caution: Always be careful around animals that may bite or sting. Do not handle animals that are unfamiliar to you.

3. Write down everything you notice about each animal. What kind of animal is it? What does it look like? How big is it? What is it doing? You may want to draw a picture of it.

Analysis

4. Compare the animals that you studied. How are they similar? How are they different?

5. How do the animals move? Did you see them communicating with other animals or defending themselves?

6. Can you tell what each animal eats? What characteristics of each animal help it find or catch food?

Terms to Learn

vertebrate   tissue
invertebrate   organ
embryo   consumer

What You'll Do

◆ Describe the differences between vertebrates and invertebrates.
◆ Explain the characteristics of animals.

What Is an Animal?

What do you think of when you hear the word *animal*? You may think of your dog or cat. You may think about giraffes or grizzly bears or other creatures you've seen in zoos or on television. But would you think about a sponge? Natural bath sponges, like the one in **Figure 1,** are the remains of an animal that lived in the ocean!

Animals come in many different shapes and sizes. Some have four legs and fur, but most do not. Some are too small to be seen without a microscope, and others are bigger than a car. But they are all part of the fascinating world of animals.

The Animal Kingdom

Scientists have named about 1 million species of animals. How many different kinds of animals do you see in **Figure 2**? It may surprise you to learn that in addition to sponges, sea anemones and corals are also animals. So are spiders, fish, birds, and dolphins. Slugs, whales, kangaroos, and humans are animals too. Scientists have divided all these animal species into about 35 phyla and classes.

Most animals look nothing like humans. However, we do share characteristics with a group of animals called vertebrates. Any animal with a skull and a backbone is a **vertebrate.** Vertebrates include fishes, amphibians, reptiles, birds, and mammals.

Figure 1 *This natural sponge used to be alive.*

Figure 2 *All of the living things in this picture are classified as animals. Do they look like animals to you?*

Even though you are probably most familiar with vertebrates, we are definitely the minority among living things. Less than five percent of known animal species are vertebrates. Take a look at **Figure 3.** As you can see, the great majority of known animal species are insects, snails, jellyfish, worms, and other **invertebrates,** animals without backbones. In fact, more than one-fourth of all animal species are beetles!

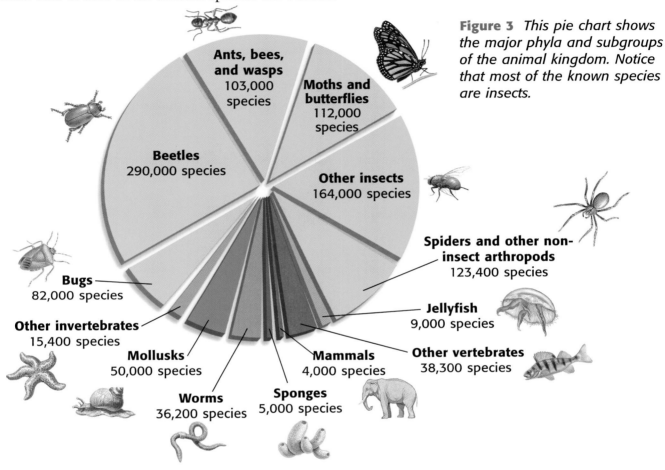

Figure 3 *This pie chart shows the major phyla and subgroups of the animal kingdom. Notice that most of the known species are insects.*

Ants, bees, and wasps
103,000 species

Moths and butterflies
112,000 species

Beetles
290,000 species

Other insects
164,000 species

Spiders and other non-insect arthropods
123,400 species

Bugs
82,000 species

Jellyfish
9,000 species

Other invertebrates
15,400 species

Mollusks
50,000 species

Mammals
4,000 species

Other vertebrates
38,300 species

Worms
36,200 species

Sponges
5,000 species

That's an Animal?

Sponges don't look like other animals. Indeed, until about 200 years ago, most people thought sponges were plants. Earthworms don't look anything like penguins, and no one would confuse a frog for a lion. So why do we say all these things are animals? What determines whether something is an animal, a plant, or something else?

There is no single answer. But all animals share characteristics that set them apart from all other living things.

Animals have many cells. All animals are *multicellular,* which means they are made of many cells. Your own body contains about 13 trillion cells. Animal cells are eukaryotic, and they do not have cell walls. Animal cells are surrounded by cell membranes only.

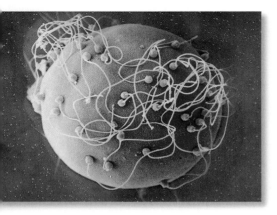

Figure 4 *Several sperm surround an egg. Only one sperm can fuse with the egg to form a new individual.*

Animals usually reproduce by sexual reproduction. Animals make sex cells, eggs or sperm. When an egg and a sperm come together at fertilization, they form the first cell of a new individual. **Figure 4** shows an egg surrounded by sperm during fertilization. Some animals, like sponges and sea stars, can also reproduce asexually, by budding or fragmentation.

Animals develop from embryos. The fertilized egg cell divides into many different cells to form an embryo. An **embryo** is an organism in the earliest stage of development. A mouse embryo is shown in **Figure 5.**

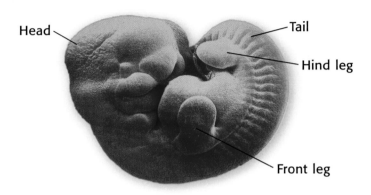

Head   Tail   Hind leg   Front leg

Figure 5   A Mouse Embryo

✔ Self-Check

Why are humans classified as vertebrates? (See page 152 to check your answer.)

Animals have many specialized parts. An animal's body has distinct parts that do different things. When a fertilized egg cell divides into many cells to form an embryo, the cells become different from each other. Some may become skin cells. Others may become muscle cells, nerve cells, or bone cells. These different kinds of cells arrange themselves to form **tissues,** which are collections of similar cells. For example, muscle cells form muscle tissue, and nerve cells form nerve tissue.

Most animals also have organs. An **organ** is a combination of two or more tissues. Your heart, lungs, and kidneys are all organs. All animals, including the shark shown in **Figure 6,** have different organs for different jobs.

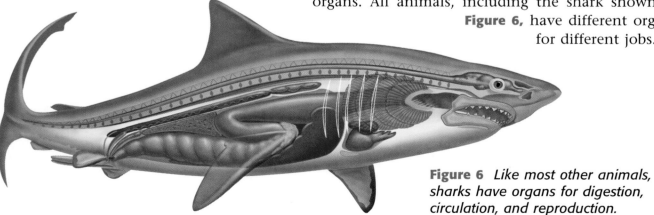

Figure 6 *Like most other animals, sharks have organs for digestion, circulation, and reproduction.*

Animals move. Most animals can move from place to place. As shown in **Figure 7,** they fly, run, swim, and jump. While it's true that other organisms move, animals are more likely to move quickly in a single direction. Some animals do not move much, though. Sea anemones and clams, for example, attach to rocks or the ocean floor and wait for food to arrive. But most animals are active.

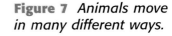
Figure 7 *Animals move in many different ways.*

Animals are consumers. Animals cannot make their own food. All animals survive by eating other organisms, parts of other organisms, or the products of other organisms. In other words, animals are consumers. A **consumer** is an organism that eats other organisms. This trait sets animals apart from plants. Except for the Venus' flytrap and a handful of other plants, plants do not eat other living things. Plants make their own food.

Animal food is as varied as animals themselves. Rabbits and caterpillars eat plants. Lions and spiders eat other animals. Reindeer eat lichens. Mosquitoes drink blood. Butterflies drink nectar from flowers.

internet **connect**

SC*i*LINKS
NSTA

TOPIC: Vertebrates and Invertebrates
GO TO: www.scilinks.org
*sci*LINKS NUMBER: HSTL330

SECTION REVIEW

1. What characteristics separate animals from plants?

2. How are tissues and organs related?

3. **Interpreting Illustrations** What characteristics of the chameleon shown at far right tell you it is an animal?

Terms to Learn

predator	hibernation
prey	estivation
innate behavior	biological clock
learned behavior	circadian rhythm

What You'll Do

- Explain the difference between learned and innate behavior.
- Explain the difference between hibernation and estivation.
- Give examples of how a biological clock influences behavior.
- Describe circadian rhythms.
- Explain how animals navigate.

Animal Behavior

In the last section, you learned the characteristics that help us recognize an animal. One characteristic of most animals is that they move. Animals jump, run, fly, dart, scurry, slither, and glide. But animals don't move just for the sake of moving. They move for a reason. They run from enemies. They climb for food. They build homes. Even the tiniest mite can actively stalk its dinner, battle for territory, or migrate. All of these activities are known as behavior.

Survival Behavior

In order to stay alive, an animal has to do many things. It must find food and water, avoid being eaten, and have a place to live. Animals have many behaviors that help them accomplish these tasks.

Looking for Lunch Animals use many different methods to find or catch food. Owls swoop down on unsuspecting mice. Bees fly from flower to flower collecting nectar. Koala bears climb trees to get eucalyptus leaves. Jellyfish harpoon and lasso their prey with their tentacles. Some animals, such as the chimpanzee shown in **Figure 8,** use tools to get dinner. Whatever the meal of choice, animals have adapted to their surroundings so that they can obtain the most food using the least amount of energy.

How to Avoid Being Eaten Animals that eat other animals are known as **predators.** The animal being eaten is the **prey.** At any given moment, an animal *diner* can become another animal's *dinner.* Therefore, animals looking for food often have to think about other things besides which food looks or tastes the best. Animals will pass up a good meal if it's too dangerous to get. But being careful is just one method of defense. Keep reading to find out what other things animals do to stay alive.

Figure 8 *Chimpanzees make and use tools in order to get ants and other food out of hard-to-reach places.*

Hiding Out One way to avoid being eaten is to be hard to see. A rabbit often "freezes" so that its natural color blends into a background of shrubs or grass. Blending in with the background is called *camouflage*. Many animals mimic twigs, leaves, stones, bark, or other materials in their environment. The insect called a walking stick looks just like a twig. Some walking sticks even sway a bit, as though a breeze were blowing. See **Figure 9** for another example of camouflage.

In Your Face The horns of a bull and the spines of a porcupine clearly signal trouble to a potential predator, but other defenses may not be as obvious. For example, animals may defend themselves with chemicals. The skunk and the bombardier beetle both spray predators with irritating chemicals. Bees, ants, and wasps inject a powerful acid into their attackers. The skin of both the South American dart-poison frog and the hooded pitohui bird of New Guinea contains a deadly toxin. Any predator that eats, or even tries to eat, one of these animals will likely die.

Warning! Animals with a chemical defense need a way to warn predators that they should look elsewhere for a meal. Their chemical weapons are often advertised by the animal's outer covering, which has a bright design called *warning coloration*, as shown in **Figure 10.** Predators will avoid any animal with the colors and patterns they associate with pain, illness, or other unpleasant experiences. The most common warning colors are vivid shades of red, yellow, orange, black, and white.

Figure 9 *This is a picture of a caterpillar camouflaged as a twig. Can you find the caterpillar?*

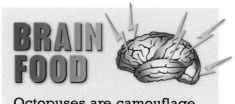

BRAIN FOOD

Octopuses are camouflage experts. They can change the color of their entire body in less than 1 second.

Figure 10 *The warning coloration of the hooded pitohui warns predators that it is poisonous. The yellow and black stripes of the stinging yellow jacket are another example.*

Why Do They Behave That Way?

How do animals know when a situation is dangerous? How do predators know which warning coloration to avoid? Sometimes animals instinctively know what to do, but sometimes they have to learn. Biologists call these two kinds of animal behavior innate behavior and learned behavior.

What did the bumblebee do to Aunt Flossie? Find out on page 124.

It's in the Genes Behavior that doesn't depend on learning or experience is known as **innate behavior.** Innate behaviors are influenced by genes. Humans inherit genes that give us the ability to walk. Puppies inherit the tendency to chew, bees the tendency to fly, and earthworms the tendency to burrow.

Some innate behaviors are present at birth. Newborn whales all have the innate ability to swim. Other innate behaviors develop months or years after birth. For example, the tendency of a bird to sing is innate. But a bird does not sing until it is nearly grown.

Animal School Just because a behavior is innate does not mean that it cannot be modified. Learning can change innate behavior. **Learned behavior** is behavior that has been learned from experience or from observing other animals. Humans inherit the tendency to speak. But the language we speak is not inherited. We might learn English, Spanish, Chinese, or Tagalog.

Humans are not the only animals that modify inherited behaviors through learning. Nearly all animals can learn. For example, many young animals learn by watching their parents. **Figure 11** shows a monkey that learned a new behavior by observation.

Figure 11 *One Japanese macaque washed the sand off a sweet potato it found on the beach. Now all of the macaques on the island wash their potatoes.*

SECTION REVIEW

1. How do innate behavior and learned behavior differ?

2. **Applying Concepts** How does the effectiveness of warning coloration for protection depend on learning?

Seasonal Behavior

In many places, animals must deal with the winter hardships of little food and bitter cold. Some avoid winter by traveling to places that are warmer. Others collect and store food. Frogs bury themselves in mud, and insects burrow into the ground.

World Travelers When food is scarce because of winter or drought, many animals migrate. To *migrate* is to travel from one place to another. Animals migrate to find food, water, or safe nesting grounds. Whales, salmon, bats, and even chimpanzees migrate. Each winter, monarch butterflies, shown in **Figure 12,** gather in central Mexico from all over North America to wait for spring. And each year, birds in the Northern Hemisphere fly thousands of kilometers south. In the spring, they return north to nest.

Slowing Down Some animals deal with food and water shortages by hibernating. **Hibernation** is a period of inactivity and decreased body temperature that some animals experience in winter. Hibernating animals survive on stored body fat. Many animals hibernate, including mice, squirrels, and skunks. While an animal hibernates, its temperature, heart rate, and breathing rate drop. Some hibernating animals drop their body temperature to a few degrees above freezing and do not wake for weeks at a time. Other animals, like the polar bears in **Figure 13,** do not enter deep hibernation. Their body temperature does not drop as severely, and they sleep for shorter periods of time.

Winter is not the only time that resources can be scarce. Many desert squirrels and mice experience a similar internal slowdown in the hottest part of the summer, when they run low on water and food. This period of reduced activity in the summer is called **estivation.**

Figure 12 *When the monarchs gather in Mexico, there can be as many as 4 million butterflies per acre!*

Don't wake the bats!

Read about the effects of humans on bat hibernation on page 24.

Figure 13 *Bears do not enter deep hibernation. However, they have periods of inactivity in which they do not eat, and their body functions slow down.*

The Rhythms of Life

Humans need clocks and calendars to tell us when to get up and go to school, when a movie starts, and when it is someone's birthday. Other animals need to know when to store food and when to fly south for the winter. The internal clocks and calendars that animals use are called biological clocks. A **biological clock** is the internal control of natural cycles. Animals may use clues from their surroundings, such as the length of the day and the temperature, to set their clocks.

Some biological clocks keep track of very small amounts of time. Other biological clocks control daily cycles. These daily cycles are called **circadian rhythms.** *Circadian* means "around the day." Most animals wake up at about the same time each day and get sleepy at about the same time each night. This is an example of a circadian rhythm.

Some biological clocks control even longer cycles. Seasonal cycles are nearly universal among animals. Animals hibernate at certain times of the year and breed at other times. And every spring, migrating birds head north. Biological clocks control all of these cycles.

How Do Animals Find Their Way?

If you were planning a trip, you'd probably consult a map. If you were hiking, you might rely on a compass or trail markers to find your way. When it's time to migrate, how do animals, such as the arctic terns in **Figure 14,** know which way to go? They must *navigate*, or find their way from one place to another.

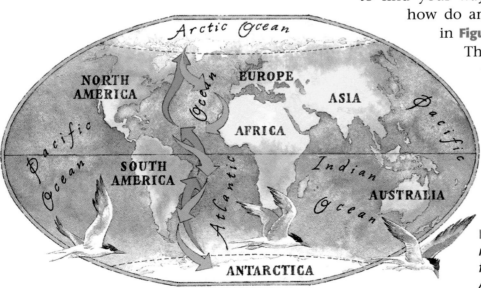

Figure 14 *Each year, arctic terns make a 38,000 km round trip from the Northern Hemisphere to Antarctica.*

Jet Lag

When people travel to places that are in a different time zone, they frequently suffer from "jet lag." Here's an example: New York time is 6 hours behind Paris time. A traveler from New York who is staying in Paris is suffering from jet lag. She goes to bed at 10 P.M., Paris time, but she wakes up at midnight, unable to fall back asleep. She lies awake all night and finally falls asleep at about 6 A.M., one hour before her alarm rings. How might circadian rhythms explain her jet lag? When it is 10 P.M. in Paris, what time is it in New York?

Take a Left at the Post Office For short trips, many animals, including humans, use landmarks to navigate. *Landmarks* are fixed objects that an animal uses to find its way. For example, once you see the corner gas station six blocks from your house, you know how to go the rest of the way. The gas station is a landmark for you.

Bees and pigeons have a kind of mental map of landmarks in their home territory. Birds use mountain ranges, rivers, and coastlines to find their way home. Humans and other animals also navigate short distances by using a mental image of an area. Not all landmarks are visual. Blind people can navigate precisely through a familiar house because they know where everything is and how long it takes to cross a room. Pigeons navigate in their home area based on smell as well as sight.

Compass Anyone? Like human sailors, animals use the position of the sun and stars as a map. But some animals, such as migratory birds, have other methods of finding their way. They navigate using the Earth's magnetic field. You can read about this in the Physics Connection at right.

Physics
CONNECTION

Earth's core acts as a giant magnet, with magnetic north and south poles. The strength and direction of the Earth's magnetic field varies from place to place, and many birds use this variation as a map. Some migratory birds have tiny magnetic crystals of magnetite in their heads above their nostrils. Biologists think that the crystals somehow move or stimulate nerves so that a bird knows its position.

SECTION REVIEW

1. Why do animals migrate?

2. What are three methods animals use to navigate?

3. How are hibernation and estivation similar? How are they different?

4. **Applying Concepts** Some research suggests that jet lag can be overcome by getting plenty of exposure to sunlight in the new time zone. Why might this method work?

internet **connect**

*SCi*LINKS.
NSTA

TOPIC: Animal Behavior, The Rhythms of Life
GO TO: www.scilinks.org
*sci*LINKS NUMBER: HSTL335, HSTL340

Terms to Learn

social behavior
communication
territory
pheromone

What You'll Do

◆ Discuss ways that animals communicate.

◆ List the advantages and disadvantages of living in groups.

Living Together

Most animals do not live alone; they associate with other animals. When animals interact, it may be in large groups or one on one. Animals may work together, or they may compete with one another. All of this behavior is called social behavior. **Social behavior** is the interaction between animals of the same species. Whether friendly or hostile, all social behavior requires communication.

Communication

Imagine what life would be like if people could not talk or read. There would be no telephones, no televisions, no books, and no Internet. The world would certainly be a lot different! Language is an important way for humans to communicate. In **communication**, a signal must travel from one animal to another, and the receiver of the signal must respond in some way.

Communication helps animals live together, find food, avoid enemies, and protect their homes. Animals communicate to warn others of danger, to identify family members, to frighten predators, and to find mates. Some of the most dramatic uses of communication are courtship displays. *Courtship* is special behavior by animals of the same species that leads to mating. **Figure 15** shows two cranes performing a courtship display.

Animals also communicate to protect their living space. Many animals defend a **territory,** an area that is occupied by one animal or a group of animals and that other members of the species are excluded from. Many species, such as the wolves in **Figure 16,** use their territories for mating, finding food, and raising young.

Figure 15 *Japanese ground cranes perform an elaborate courtship dance.*

Figure 16 *These wolves are howling to discourage neighboring wolves from invading their territory.*

How Do Animals Communicate?

Animals communicate by signaling intentions and information to other animals through smell, sound, vision, and touch. Most animal signals tend to be simple compared with those that we use. But no matter which signal is used, it must convey specific information.

Do You Smell Trouble? One method of communication is chemical. Even single-celled organisms communicate with one another by means of chemicals. In animals, these chemicals are called **pheromones** (FER uh MOHNZ).

Ants and other insects secrete a variety of pheromones. For example, alarm substances released into the air alert other members of the species to danger. Trail substances are left along a path so that others can follow to find food and return to the nest. Recognition odors on an ant's body announce which colony an ant is from. Such a message signals both friends and enemies, depending on who is receiving the message.

Many animals, including vertebrates, use pheromones to attract or influence members of the opposite sex. Amazingly, elephants and insects use some of the same pheromones to attract mates. Queen butterflies, like the one in **Figure 17,** use pheromones during their courtship displays.

Figure 17 *Queen butterflies use pheromones as part of their courtship display.*

Do You Hear What I Hear? Animals also communicate by making noises. Wolves howl. Dolphins and whales use whistles and complex clicking noises to communicate with others. Male birds may sing songs in the spring to claim their territory or attract a mate.

Sound is a signal that can reach a large number of animals over a large area. Elephants communicate with other elephants kilometers away using rumbles at a frequency too low for most humans to hear, as described in **Figure 18.** Humpback whales sing songs that can be heard for kilometers.

Figure 18 *Elephants communicate with low-pitched sounds that humans cannot hear. When an elephant is communicating this way, the skin on its forehead flutters.*

Figure 19 *When dogs want to play, they drop down on their forelegs.*

Showing Off Many forms of communication are visual. When we wink at a friend or frown at an opponent, we are communicating with *body language.* Other animals are no different. **Figure 19** shows one way dogs use body language.

An animal that wants to scare another animal may do something that makes it appear larger. It may ruffle its feathers or fur or open its mouth and show its teeth. Visual displays are also important in courtship. Fireflies blink complex signals in the dark to attract one another.

Getting in Touch An animal may also use touch to communicate, like the honeybee does. A honeybee that finds a patch of flowers rich in nectar returns to its hive to tell fellow workers where the flowers are. Inside the dark hive, the bee communicates by performing a complex figure-eight dance, as shown below, which the other bees learn by observation and touch.

The Dance of the Bees

Honeybees do a "waggle dance" to tell other bees where they've found nectar. As the bee goes through the middle of the figure eight, it communicates two things: the direction of the nectar and the distance to the nectar from the hive. Other worker bees gather closely around the dancing bee to learn the dance. By learning the dance, the bees learn the direction to the nectar.

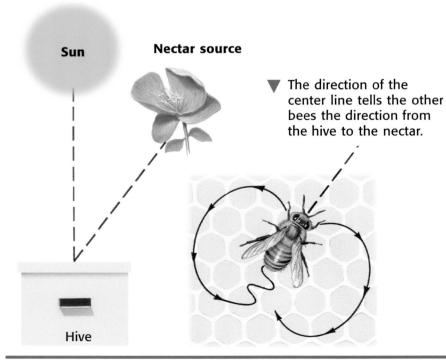

Sun

Nectar source

▼ The direction of the center line tells the other bees the direction from the hive to the nectar.

Hive

▲ As the bee goes through the center, it waggles its abdomen. The number of waggles tells the other bees how far away the nectar is.

Part of the Family

Tigers live alone. Except for the time a mother tiger spends with her cubs, a tiger meets other tigers rarely and for very short periods. Yet the tiger's closest relative, the lion, is rarely alone. Lions live in groups called prides. The members of a pride sleep together, hunt together, and raise their cubs together. **Figure 20** shows two lions at work. Why do some animals live in groups, while others live apart?

Figure 20 *This pair of lions cooperates to hunt a gazelle.*

The Benefits of Living in a Group Living with other animals is much safer than living alone. Large groups can spot a predator or other dangers quickly, and groups of animals can cooperate to defend themselves. For example, if a predator threatens them, a herd of musk oxen will circle their young with their horns pointed outward. Honeybees attack by the thousands when another animal tries to take their honey.

Living together can also help animals find food. Tigers and other animals that hunt alone can usually kill only animals that are smaller than themselves. In contrast, lions, wolves, hyenas, and other predators that hunt cooperatively can kill much larger prey.

The Downside of Living in a Group Living in groups causes problems as well. Animals living in groups attract predators, so they must always be on the lookout, as shown in **Figure 21**. Groups of animals need more food, and animals in groups compete with each other for food and for mates. Individuals in groups can also give each other diseases.

Figure 21 *A ground squirrel whistles a loud alarm to alert other ground squirrels that danger is near.*

SECTION REVIEW

1. Scientists have discovered pheromones in humans. Name three other types of animal communication used by humans.

2. Why is communication important? Name three reasons.

3. **Applying Concepts** Considering what you have learned about group living, list two advantages and two disadvantages to living in a group of humans.

internetconnect

*sci*LINKS.
NSTA

TOPIC: Communication in the Animal Kingdom
GO TO: www.scilinks.org
*sci***LINKS NUMBER:** HSTL345

Discovery Lab

Wet, Wiggly Worms!

Earthworms have been digging in the earth for more than 100 million years! Earthworms fertilize the soil with their waste and loosen the soil when they tunnel through the moist dirt of a garden or lawn. Worms are food for many animals, such as birds, frogs, snakes, rodents, and fish. Some say they are good food for people, too!

In this activity, you will observe the behavior of a live earthworm. Remember that earthworms are living animals that deserve to be handled gently. Be sure to keep your earthworm moist during this activity. The skin of the earthworm must stay moist so that the worm can get oxygen. If the earthworm's skin dries out, the worm will suffocate and die. Use a spray bottle to moisten the earthworm with water.

MATERIALS

- spray bottle
- dissecting pan
- paper towels
- water
- live earthworm
- probe
- celery leaves
- flashlight
- shoe box with lid
- clock
- soil
- metric ruler

Procedure

1. Place a wet paper towel in the bottom of a dissecting pan. Put a live earthworm on the paper towel, and observe how the earthworm moves. Record your observations in your ScienceLog.

2. Use the probe to carefully touch the anterior end (head) of the worm. Gently touch other areas of the worm's body with the probe. Record the kinds of responses you observe.

3. Shine a flashlight on the anterior end of the earthworm. Record the earthworm's reaction to the light.

4. Place celery leaves at one end of the pan. Record how the earthworm responds to the presence of food.

5. Line the bottom of the shoe box with a damp paper towel. Cover half of the shoe box with the box top.

6. Place the worm on the uncovered side of the shoe box in the light. Record your observations of the worm's behavior for 3 minutes.

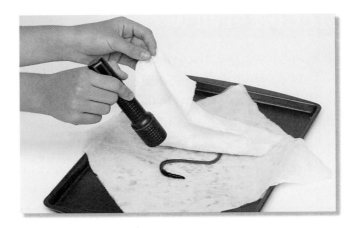

7 Place the worm in the covered side of the box. Record your observations for 3 minutes.

8 Repeat steps 6–7 three times.

9 Spread some loose soil evenly in the bottom of the shoe box so that it is about 4 cm deep. Place the earthworm on top of the soil. Observe and record the earthworm's behavior for 3 minutes.

10 Dampen the soil on one side of the box, and leave the other side dry. Place the earthworm in the center of the box between the wet and dry soil. Cover the box, and wait 3 minutes. Uncover the box, and record your observations. Repeat this procedure 3 times. (You may need to search for the worm!)

Analysis

11 How did the earthworm respond to being touched? Were some areas more sensitive than others?

12 How is the earthworm's behavior influenced by light? Based on your observations, describe how an animal's response to a stimulus might provide protection for the animal.

13 How did the earthworm respond to the presence of food?

14 When the worm was given a choice of wet or dry soil, which did it choose? Explain this result.

Going Further

Based on your observations of an earthworm's behavior, draw a conclusion about where you might expect to find earthworms. Prepare a poster that illustrates your conclusion. Draw a picture with colored markers, or cut out pictures from magazines. Include all the variables that you used in your experiment, such as soil or no soil, wet or dry soil, light or dark, and food. At the bottom of your poster, write a caption describing where earthworms might be found in nature.

Chapter Highlights

SECTION 1

Vocabulary

vertebrate *(p. 4)*
invertebrate *(p. 5)*
embryo *(p. 6)*
tissue *(p. 6)*
organ *(p. 6)*
consumer *(p. 7)*

Section Notes

- Animals with a skull and a backbone are vertebrates. Animals without a backbone are invertebrates.
- Animals are multicellular. Their cells are eukaryotic and lack a cell wall.
- Most animals reproduce sexually and develop from embryos.
- Most animals have tissues and organs.
- Most animals move.
- Animals are consumers.

SECTION 2

Vocabulary

predator *(p. 8)*
prey *(p. 8)*
innate behavior *(p. 10)*
learned behavior *(p. 10)*
hibernation *(p. 11)*
estivation *(p. 11)*
biological clock *(p. 12)*
circadian rhythm *(p. 12)*

Section Notes

- Many animals use camouflage, chemicals, or both to defend themselves against predators.
- Behavior may be classified as innate or learned. The potential for innate behavior is inherited. Learned behavior depends on experience.
- Some animals migrate to find food, water, or safe nesting grounds.
- Some animals hibernate in the winter, and some estivate in the summer.

☑ Skills Check

Math Concepts

TIME DIFFERENCE In the Apply on page 13, you considered how the time difference between New York and Paris could explain jet lag. Paris time is 6 hours later than New York time. If it is 10 P.M. in Paris, subtract 6 hours to get New York time.

$$10 - 6 = 4$$

It is 4 P.M. in New York. Similarly, when it is 7 A.M. in Paris, it is 1 A.M. in New York.

Visual Understanding

THE DANCE OF THE BEES The illustration on page 16 shows how bees use the waggle dance to communicate the location of a nectar source. Notice the position of the sun in relation to the hive and the nectar source. The bee communicates this information by the direction of the center line in the dance.

- Animals have internal biological clocks to control natural cycles.

- Daily cycles are called circadian rhythms.

- Some biological clocks are regulated by cues from an animal's environment.

- Animals navigate close to home using landmarks and a mental image of their home area.

- Some animals use the positions of the sun and stars or Earth's magnetic field to navigate.

Labs

Aunt Flossie and the Bumblebee *(p. 124)*

Vocabulary

social behavior *(p. 14)*

communication *(p. 14)*

territory *(p. 14)*

pheromone *(p. 15)*

Section Notes

- Communication must include both a signal and a response.

- Two important kinds of communication are courtship and territorial displays.

- Animals communicate through sight, sound, touch, and smell.

- Group living allows animals to spot both prey and predators more easily.

- Groups of animals are more visible to predators than are individuals, and animals in groups must compete with one another for food and mates.

 internetconnect

GO TO: go.hrw.com

Visit the **HRW** Web site for a variety of learning tools related to this chapter. Just type in the keyword:

KEYWORD: HSTANM

GO TO: www.scilinks.org

Visit the **National Science Teachers Association** on-line Web site for Internet resources related to this chapter. Just type in the *sci*LINKS number for more information about the topic:

TOPIC: Vertebrates and Invertebrates   *sci*LINKS **NUMBER:** HSTL330

TOPIC: Animal Behavior   *sci*LINKS **NUMBER:** HSTL335

TOPIC: The Rhythms of Life   *sci*LINKS **NUMBER:** HSTL340

TOPIC: Communication in the Animal Kingdom   *sci*LINKS **NUMBER:** HSTL345

Chapter Review

To complete the following sentences, choose the correct term from each pair of terms listed below:

1. An animal with a skull and a backbone is __?__. An animal with no backbone is __?__. *(an invertebrate* or *a vertebrate)*

2. A behavior that does not depend on experience is __?__. *(innate* or *learned)*

3. In the summer, an animal enters a state of reduced activity. The animal is __?__. *(estivating* or *hibernating)*

4. Daily cycles are known as __?__. *(biological clocks* or *circadian rhythms)*

5. When an egg and a sperm come together, they form __?__. *(an embryo* or *an organ)*

Multiple Choice

6. Which characteristic is not true of animals?
   a. They are multicellular.
   b. They usually reproduce sexually.
   c. They make their own food.
   d. They have tissues.

7. Living in groups
   a. attracts predators.
   b. helps prey spot predators.
   c. helps animals find food.
   d. All of the above

8. Warning coloration is
   a. a kind of camouflage.
   b. a way to warn predators away.
   c. always black and white.
   d. always a sign that an animal is poisonous to eat.

9. Some birds use Earth's magnetic field
   a. to attract mates.
   b. to navigate.
   c. to set their biological clocks.
   d. to defend their territory.

10. To defend against predators, an animal might use
    a. camouflage.   c. toxins.
    b. warning coloration. d. All of the above

Short Answer

11. How are pheromones used in communication?

12. What is a territory? Give an example of a territory from your own environment.

13. What landmarks help you navigate your way home from school?

14. What do migration and hibernation have in common?

Concept Mapping

15. Use the following terms to create a concept map: estivation, circadian rhythms, seasonal behaviors, hibernation, migration, biological clocks.

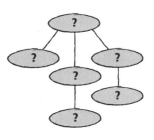

Write one or two sentences to answer the following questions:

16. If you smell a skunk while riding in a car and you shut the car window, has the skunk communicated with you? Explain.

17. Flying is an innate behavior in birds. Is it an innate behavior or a learned behavior in humans? Why?

18. Ants depend on pheromones and touch for communication, but birds depend more on sight and sound. Why might these two types of animals communicate differently?

INTERPRETING GRAPHICS

The pie chart below shows the major phyla of the animal species on Earth. Use the chart to answer the questions that follow.

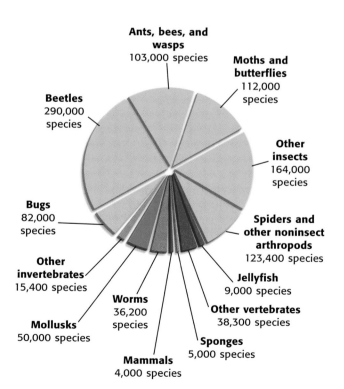

Ants, bees, and wasps
103,000 species

Moths and butterflies
112,000 species

Beetles
290,000 species

Other insects
164,000 species

Bugs
82,000 species

Spiders and other noninsect arthropods
123,400 species

Other invertebrates
15,400 species

Jellyfish
9,000 species

Worms
36,200 species

Other vertebrates
38,300 species

Mollusks
50,000 species

Sponges
5,000 species

Mammals
4,000 species

19. What group of animals has the most species? How is this shown on the chart?

20. How many species of beetles are on Earth? How does that compare with the number of mammal species?

21. How many species of vertebrates are known?

22. Scientists are still discovering new species. Which pie wedges are most likely to increase? Why do you think so?

MATH IN SCIENCE

Use the data from the pie chart to answer the following questions:

23. What is the total number of animal species on Earth?

24. How many different species of moths and butterflies are on Earth?

25. What percentage of all animal species are moths and butterflies?

26. What percentage of all animal species are vertebrates?

Reading Check-up

Take a minute to review your answers to the Pre-Reading Questions found at the bottom of page 2. Have your answers changed? If necessary, revise your answers based on what you have learned since you began this chapter.

EYE ON THE ENVIRONMENT

Do Not Disturb!

Did you know that bats are the only mammals that can fly? Unlike many birds, most bat species in the northern and central parts of the United States don't fly south for the winter. Instead of migrating, many bat species go into hibernation. But if their sleep is disturbed too often, the bats may die.

Long Winter's Nap

Most bats eat insects, but winter is a time of food shortage. In late summer, many North American bats begin to store up extra fat. These fat reserves help them survive the winter. For the stored fat to last until spring, bats must hibernate. They travel to caves where winter temperatures are low enough—0°C to 9.5°C—and stable enough for the bats to hibernate comfortably.

Hibernating bats' body temperature drops to almost the same temperature as the surrounding cave. Their heart rate, normally about 400 beats per minute, slows to about 25 beats per minute. With these changes, the stored fat will usually last all winter, unless human visitors wake the bats from their deep sleep. If that happens, the bats may starve to death.

No Admittance!

Even with their slowed metabolism, bats must wake up occasionally. They still need to drink water every so often. Sometimes they move to a warmer or cooler spot in the cave. But bats usually have enough fat stored so that they can wake up a few times each winter and then go back to sleep.

People visiting the caves force the bats to wake up unnecessarily. This causes the bats to use up the fat they have stored faster than they can afford. For example, a little brown bat consumes 67 days worth of stored fat each time it awakes. And with no insects around to eat, it cannot build up its fat reserve again.

▲ *These little brown bats are roosting in a cave.*

Most species of hibernating bats can survive the winter after waking about three extra times. But frequent intrusions can lead to the death of a whole colony of bats. Thousands of these interesting and extremely beneficial mammals may die when people carelessly or deliberately disturb them as they hibernate.

Increase Your Knowledge

▶ Using the Internet or the library, find out more about bats. Learn how they are beneficial to the environment and what threatens their survival. Discuss with your classmates some ways to protect bats and their habitats.

WEIRD SCIENCE

ANIMAL CANNIBALS

Competing, surviving, and reproducing are all part of life. And in some species, so is *cannibalism* (eating members of one's own species). But how does cannibalism relate to competing, surviving, and reproducing? It turns out that sometimes an animal's choice of food is a factor in whether its genes get passed on or not.

Picky Eaters

Tiger salamanders start life by eating zooplankton, aquatic insect larvae, and sometimes tadpoles. If conditions in their small pond include intense competition with members of their own species, some of the larger salamanders become cannibals!

Scientists are not sure why tiger salamanders become cannibals or why they usually eat nonrelatives. Scientists hypothesize that this behavior eliminates competition. By eating other salamanders, a tiger salamander reduces competition for food and improves the chances of its own survival. That increases the chances its genes will be passed on to the next generation. And eating nonrelatives helps to ensure that genes coming from the same family are more likely to be passed on to the next generation.

The Ultimate Sacrifice

Male Australian redback spiders take a different approach to making sure their genes are passed on. During mating, the male spider tumbles his body over, does a handstand, and waves his abdomen near the female's mouth, offering himself to her as a meal. The female accepts the dinner invitation if she is hungry. And it seems that about 65 percent of the time she is hungry!

Male spiders want to pass on their genes, so they compete fiercely for the females. A female redback spider wants to make sure that as many of her eggs are fertilized as possible, so she often mates with two different males. If the female eats the first male, studies show that she will not mate with a second male as often as she would if she had not eaten the first suitor. Because eating the male takes some time, more eggs are fertilized by the mate who also becomes dinner. The male spider who offers himself as a meal may then have more of his genes passed to the next generation.

▲ *During mating, male Australian redback spiders offer themselves as food to their mates.*

On Your Own

▶ Other animals devour members of their own species. Scientists believe there are a variety of reasons for the behavior. Using the Internet or the library, research cannibalism in different animals, such as praying mantises, blue crabs, stickleback fish, black widow spiders, spadefoot toad tadpoles, and lions. Present your findings to the class.

Invertebrates

Pre-Reading
Questions

1. How are sponges different from other invertebrates?

2. How are you different from an octopus? How are you similar?

A SCI-FI SLUG?

No, this isn't an alien! It's a sea slug, a close relative of garden slugs and snails. This sea slug lives in the cold Pacific Ocean near the coast of California. Its bright coloring comes from the food that the slug eats. This animal doesn't breathe with lungs. Instead, it brings oxygen into its body through the spikes on its back.

Sea slugs don't have a backbone. In this chapter, you will discover many other animals that have no backbones. You will also learn about the structure and function of their bodies.

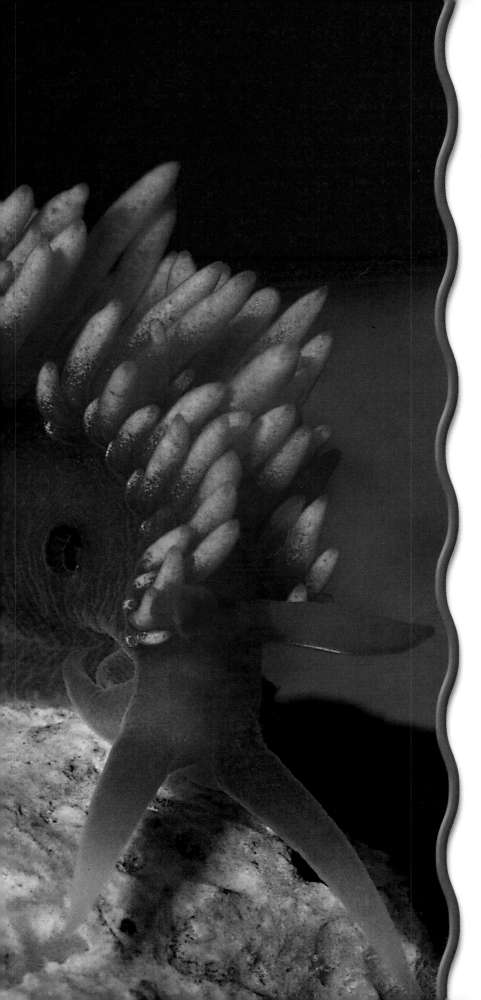

CLASSIFY IT!

Animals are classified according to their different characteristics, including their internal and external features. In this activity, you will try your hand at classification.

Procedure

1. Look at the **pictures** that your teacher has provided. Scientists group all of these animals together because these animals do not have a backbone.

2. Which animals are the most alike? Put them in the same group.

3. For each group, decide which animals within the group are the most alike. Put these animals into smaller groups inside of their larger group.

4. In your ScienceLog or using a computer, construct a table that organizes your classification groups.

Analysis

5. What features did you use to classify these animals into groups? Explain why you think these features are the most important.

6. What features did you use to place the animals in smaller groups? Explain your reasoning.

7. Compare your table with those of your classmates. What similarities or differences do you find?

Terms to Learn

invertebrate   ganglia
bilateral symmetry   gut
radial symmetry   coelom
asymmetrical

What You'll Do

◆ Describe the difference between radial and bilateral symmetry.

◆ Describe the function of a coelom.

◆ Explain how sponges are different from other animals.

◆ Describe the differences in the simple nervous systems of the cnidarians and the flatworms.

Simple Invertebrates

Animals without backbones, also known as **invertebrates,** make up an estimated 97 percent of all animal species. So far, more than 1 million invertebrates have been named. Most biologists think that millions more remain undiscovered.

Tiger beetle

No Backbones Here!

Invertebrates come in many different shapes and sizes. Grasshoppers, clams, earthworms, and jellyfish are all invertebrates, and they are all very different from each other. But one thing invertebrates have in common is that they don't have backbones.

The differences and similarities among all animals, including invertebrates, can be compared by looking at several characteristics. These characteristics include the type of body plan, the presence or absence of a head, and the way food is digested and absorbed.

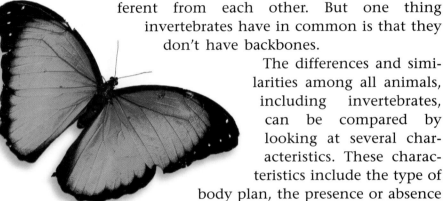

Morpho butterfly

Body Plans Invertebrates have two basic body plans, or types of *symmetry*. Symmetry can be bilateral or radial. Animal body plans are shown on the next page.

Most animals have bilateral symmetry. An animal with **bilateral symmetry** has a body with two similar halves. For example, if you draw an imaginary line down the middle of an ant, you see the same features on each side of the line.

Some invertebrates have radial symmetry. In an animal with **radial symmetry,** the body parts are arranged in a circle around a central point. If you were to draw an imaginary line across the top of a sea anemone, you would see that both halves look the same. But you could draw the line in any direction and still see two similar halves.

The simplest invertebrates, the sponges, have no symmetry at all. Animals without symmetry are **asymmetrical.**

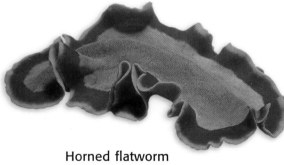

Horned flatworm

Harlequin shrimp

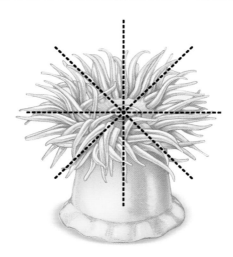

This ant has **bilateral symmetry.** The two halves of its body mirror each other. On each side you see one eye, one antenna, and three legs.

This sea anemone has **radial symmetry.** Animals with radial symmetry have a body organized around the center, like spokes on a wheel.

This sponge is **asymmetrical.** You cannot draw a straight line so that its body is divided into two equal halves.

Getting a Head All animals except sponges have fibers called *nerves* that carry signals to control the movements of their body. Simple invertebrates have nerves arranged in networks or in nerve cords throughout their body. These simple animals have no brain or head.

In some invertebrates, dozens of nerve cells come together in groups called **ganglia** (singular, *ganglion*). Ganglia occur throughout the body, controlling different body parts. **Figure 1** shows one of the ganglia, the brain, and nerve cords of a leech.

More-complex animals have a brain and a head, where the brain is stored. The brain controls many different nerves in different parts of the body.

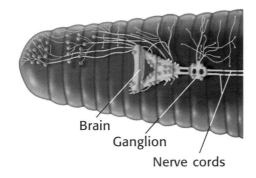

Brain
Ganglion
Nerve cords

Figure 1 *Leeches have a simple brain and ganglia. A pair of nerve cords connects the brain and ganglia.*

Don't You Have Any Guts? Almost all animals digest food in a central gut. The **gut** is a pouch lined with cells that release powerful enzymes. These enzymes break down food into small particles that cells can then absorb. Your gut is your digestive tract.

Complex animals have a special space in the body for the gut. This space is the **coelom** (SEE luhm), shown in **Figure 2.** The coelum allows the gut to move food without interference from the movements of the body. Other organs, such as the heart and lungs, are also in the coelom, but they are separated from the gut.

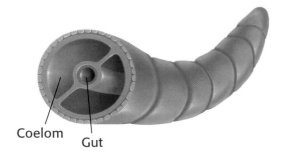

Coelom
Gut

Figure 2 *This is the coelom of an earthworm. The gut and organs are in this special cavity.*

Sponges

Sponges are the simplest animals. They have no symmetry, no head or nerves, and no gut. Although sponges can move, they are so slow that their movement is very difficult to see. In fact, sponges were once thought to be plants. But sponges cannot make their own food and must eat other organisms. That's one reason they are classified as animals.

Kinds of Sponges All sponges live in water, and most are found in the ocean. As shown in **Figure 3,** they come in beautiful colors and a variety of shapes.

Most sponges have a skeleton made of needlelike splinters called *spicules,* as shown in **Figure 4.** Spicules come in many shapes, from simple, straight needles to curved rods and complex star shapes. The skeleton supports the body of the sponge and helps protect it from predators.

Sponges are divided into classes according to the type of spicules they have. The largest class of sponges contain spicules made of silicate, the material we use to make glass. Bath sponges are similar to silica sponges, but they lack spicules. Instead of spicules, they have a skeleton made of a protein called *spongin.* That is why they are soft. Another group of sponges have spicules made of calcium carbonate, the material that makes up the shells of shellfish.

Re-form and Replace If a sponge's body is broken apart by being forced through a sieve, the separate cells will come back together and re-form the same sponge. In addition, new sponges can form from pieces broken off another sponge. Unlike most animals, a sponge can also replace its body parts, or *regenerate.*

Giant barrel sponge

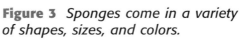

Figure 3 *Sponges come in a variety of shapes, sizes, and colors.*

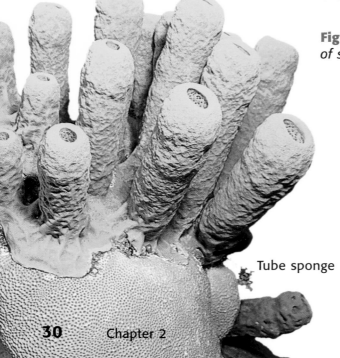

Tube sponge

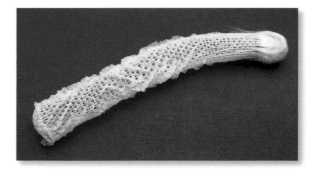

Figure 4 *This is the skeleton of a glass sponge.*

How Do Sponges Eat? Sponges belong to the phylum Porifera. The name refers to the thousands of holes, or *pores,* on the outside of sponges. The sponge sweeps water into its body through these pores. Inside the body, cells called *collar cells* filter food particles and microorganisms from the water. The rest of the water flows into a central cavity and out a hole at the top of the sponge, like smoke going up a chimney. The hole at the top is called the *osculum.* **Figure 5** shows this process.

Sponges don't have a gut. Instead, each collar cell digests its own particles of food. No other animal has anything like collar cells.

Collar cells line the central cavity of a sponge. Each collar cell filters particles of food from the water and digests them.

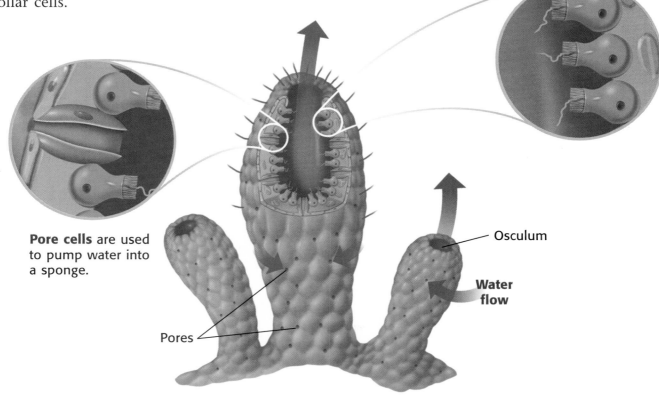

Pore cells are used to pump water into a sponge.

Pores

Osculum

Water flow

Figure 5 *A sponge filters particles of food from water using collar cells and then pumps the water out the osculum. A sponge can filter up to 22 L of water a day.*

SECTION REVIEW

1. Why are collar cells important in classifying sponges as animals?

2. What is a coelom?

3. **Interpreting Graphics** Does the animal shown at right have radial symmetry, bilateral symmetry, or no symmetry? Explain your answer.

Jellyfish

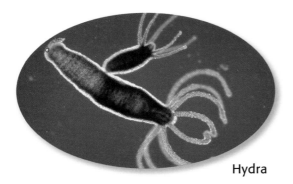
Hydra

Figure 6 *These three organisms are cnidarians. Why are they in the same phylum?*

Sea anemone

Cnidarians

Take a look at the organisms shown in **Figure 6.** They look very different, but all of these animals belong to the phylum Cnidaria (ni DER ee uh).

The word *cnidaria* comes from the Greek word for "nettle." Nettles are plants that release stinging barbs into the skin. Cnidarians do the same. All cnidarians have stinging cells. Do you know anyone who has been stung by a jellyfish? It is a very painful experience!

Cnidarians are more complex than sponges. Cnidarians have complex tissues, a gut for digesting food, and a nervous system. However, some species of cnidarians do share a characteristic with sponges. If the cells of the body are separated, they can come back together to form the cnidarian.

The Medusa and the Polyp Cnidarians come in two forms, the medusa and the polyp. They are shown in **Figure 7.** The *medusa* looks like a mushroom with tentacles streaming down from below. A well-known medusa is the jellyfish. As a medusa's body, or bell, contracts and relaxes, the medusa swims through the water.

The other cnidarian body form is the *polyp*. Polyps are shaped like vases and usually live attached to a surface.

Some cnidarians are polyps and medusas at different times in their life. But most cnidarians spend their life as a polyp.

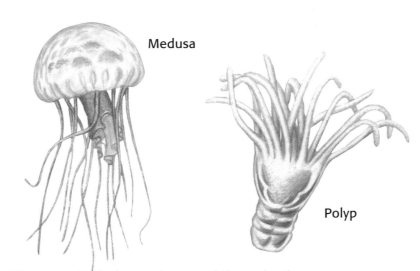
Medusa

Polyp

Figure 7 *Both the medusa and the polyp have radial symmetry. Can you see why?*

Kinds of Cnidarians There are three classes of cnidarians: hydras, jellyfish, and sea anemones and corals. Hydras are common cnidarians that live in fresh water. They spend their entire life in the polyp form. Jellyfish spend most of their life as a medusa.

Sea anemones and corals are polyps all their life. They look like brightly colored flowers. Corals are tiny cnidarians that live in colonies. These colonies build huge skeletons of calcium carbonate. Each new generation of corals builds on top of the last generation. Over thousands of years, these tiny animals build massive underwater reefs. Coral reefs can be found in warm tropical waters throughout the world.

Catching Lunch All cnidarians have long tentacles covered with special stinging cells. When a small fish or other organism brushes against the tentacles of a cnidarian, hundreds of stinging cells fire into the organism and release a paralyzing toxin. Each stinging cell uses water pressure to fire a tiny barbed spear called a *nematocyst* (ne MA toh sist). **Figure 8** shows a nematocyst before and after firing.

Environment CONNECTION

Coral reefs, some of which are more than 2.5 million years old, are home to one-fourth of all marine fish species. Unfortunately, living coral reefs are threatened by overfishing, pollution, mining, and accidental damage from swimmers and boats. Scientists are now looking for ways to help protect coral reefs.

Figure 8 *Each stinging cell contains a nematocyst.*

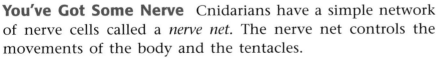

Before firing Coiled inside each stinging cell is a tiny barbed harpoon.

After firing When the nematocyst is fired, the long barbed strand ejects into the water. Larger barbs also cover the base of the strand.

You've Got Some Nerve Cnidarians have a simple network of nerve cells called a *nerve net*. The nerve net controls the movements of the body and the tentacles.

A medusa has a *nerve ring* in the center of its nerve net. This ring of nerve cells coordinates the swimming of a jellyfish in the same way that our spinal cord coordinates walking. The nerve ring is not a brain, however. Cnidarians do not think or plan in the way that more-complex animals do.

Self-Check

Medusas have a nerve ring, but polyps do not. How does the way medusas move explain their more complex nervous system? *(See page 152 to check your answer.)*

Flatworms

When you think of worms, you probably think of earthworms. But there are many other types of worms, and most of them are too tiny to see. The simplest group of worms are the flatworms.

Look at the flatworm shown in **Figure 9.** Unlike the invertebrates you have studied so far, flatworms have bilateral symmetry. Most flatworms also have a clearly defined head and two large, unblinking eyespots. Even though the eyespots cannot focus, a flatworm knows the direction that light is coming from. A flatworm also has two bumps on each side of its head. These are *sensory lobes* and are used for detecting food.

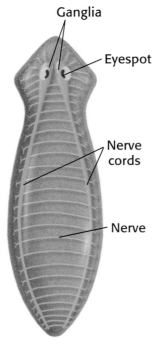

Figure 9 *This flatworm is called a planarian. It has a head with eyespots and sensory lobes.*

Ganglia

Eyespot

Nerve cords

Nerve

Figure 10 *The nervous system of a flatworm has nerves connecting two parallel nerve cords. Ganglia make up a primitive brain.*

Planarians Flatworms are divided into three classes. The big-eyed flatworms we have been discussing are called *planarians.* Most of these flatworms are small; their length is less than the length of a fingernail. They live in water and on land. Most planarians are predators. They eat other animals or parts of other animals and digest food in their gut. The planarian's head, eyespots, and sensory lobes are clues that it has a brain for processing information. **Figure 10** shows a diagram of the nervous system of a planarian.

Flukes and Tapeworms The two other groups of flatworms are *flukes* and *tapeworms.* A fluke is shown in **Figure 11.** These animals are parasites. A *parasite* is an organism that feeds on another living creature, called the *host.* The host is usually not killed. Most flukes and all tapeworms find their way inside the bodies of other animals, where they live and reproduce. Fertilized eggs pass out of the host's body with the body's waste. If these fertilized eggs end up in drinking water or on food, they can be eaten by another host, where they will develop into a new fluke or tapeworm.

Figure 11 *Flukes use suckers to attach to their host.*

Flukes and tapeworms have tiny heads without eyespots or sensory lobes. They have special suckers and hooks for attaching to the host. Those flatworms that live inside the gut of their host have special skin that resists digestion by the stomach enzymes of the host. Tapeworms are so specialized that they have no gut at all. These creatures simply absorb nutrients from the intestines of their host. **Figure 12** shows a tapeworm that can infect humans.

Roundworms

Roundworms, or nematodes, are round when viewed in cross section and are long and slender. Like other worms, they have bilateral symmetry. Most species of roundworms are tiny. A single rotten apple lying on the ground in an orchard could contain 100,000 roundworms. These tiny creatures break down the dead tissues of plants and animals and help build rich soils. **Figure 13** shows a roundworm.

Roundworms have a simple nervous system. A ring of ganglia forms a primitive brain, and parallel nerve cords run the length of their body.

Most roundworms are parasites. Roundworms that infect humans include pinworms and hookworms. Another roundworm is passed from infected pork to humans and causes trichinosis (TRIK i NOH sis), a severe illness. Cooking pork thoroughly will kill the roundworms.

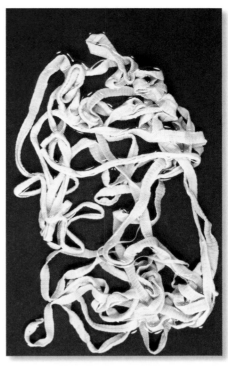

Figure 12 *Tapeworms can reach enormous sizes. Some can grow longer than a school bus!*

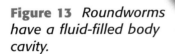

Figure 13 *Roundworms have a fluid-filled body cavity.*

SECTION REVIEW

1. What characteristic gives cnidarians their name?

2. What are two characteristics of flatworms that make them different from cnidarians?

3. **Analyzing Relationships** Both predators and parasites live off the tissues of other animals. Explain the difference between a predator and a parasite.

internet**connect**

SC*i*LINKS
NSTA

TOPIC: Sponges, Roundworms
GO TO: www.scilinks.org
*sci***LINKS NUMBER:** HSTL355, HSTL360

Terms to Learn

open circulatory system
closed circulatory system
segment

What You'll Do

◆ Describe the body parts of a mollusk.

◆ Explain the difference between an open circulatory system and a closed circulatory system.

◆ Describe segmentation.

Mollusks and Annelid Worms

Have you ever eaten clam chowder or calamari? Have you ever seen worms on the sidewalk after it rains? If you have, then you have encountered the invertebrates discussed in this section—mollusks and annelid worms. These invertebrates are more complex than the invertebrates you have read about so far. Mollusks and annelid worms have a coelom and a circulatory system. And they have more-complex nervous systems than those of the flatworms and roundworms.

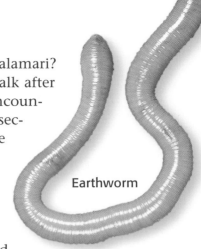

Earthworm

Mollusks

The phylum Mollusca includes snails, slugs, clams, oysters, squids, and octopuses. The mollusks are the second largest phylum of animals. Most mollusks are in three classes: *gastropods* (slugs and snails), *bivalves* (clams and other two-shelled shellfish), and *cephalopods* (squids and octopuses). **Figure 14** shows some of the variety of mollusks.

Snails

Squid

Clam

Figure 14 *A snail, a squid, and a clam are all mollusks. Snails are gastropods; squids are cephalopods; and clams are bivalves.*

Most mollusks live in the ocean, but some live in freshwater habitats. Other mollusks, such as slugs and snails, have adapted to life on land.

Mollusks range in size from 1 mm long snails to the giant squid, which can reach up to 18 m in length. Most mollusks move slowly, but some squids can swim up to 40 km/h and leap more than 4 m above the water.

$\div \ 5 \ \div \ ^{\Omega} \ _{\le} \ ^{\infty} \ + _{\Omega} \ ^{\vee} \ 9 \ _{\infty} \ ^{\le} \ \Sigma \ 2$

MATH **BREAK**

Speeding Squid

If a squid is swimming at 30 km/h, how far can it go in 1 minute?

How Do You Know a Mollusk When You See One? A snail, a clam, and a squid look quite different from one another. Yet on closer inspection, the bodies of all mollusks are almost the same. The body parts shared by mollusks are described in **Figure 15.**

Figure 15 *A mollusk has a soft body, usually covered by a shell. All mollusks also have a foot, a visceral mass, and a mantle.*

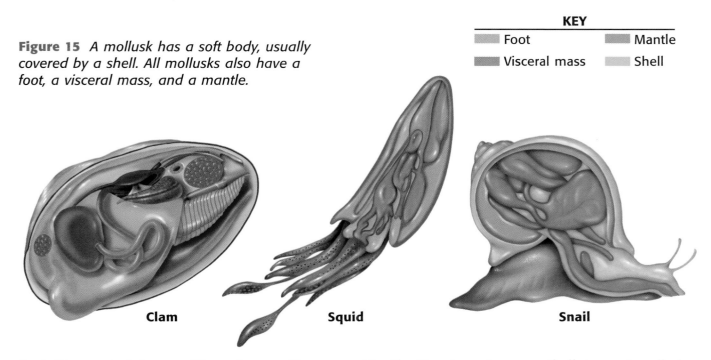

KEY

| Foot | Mantle |
| Visceral mass | Shell |

Clam   **Squid**   **Snail**

Foot The most obvious feature of a mollusk is a broad, muscular foot. A mollusk uses its foot to move. In gastropods, the foot secretes mucus that it slides along.

Visceral mass The visceral (VIS uhr uhl) mass contains the gills, gut, and other organs. It is located in a mollusk's coelom.

Mantle The visceral mass is covered by a layer of tissue called the mantle. The mantle protects the body of mollusks that do not have a shell.

Shell In most mollusks, the outside of the mantle secretes a shell. The shell protects the mollusk from predators and keeps land mollusks from drying out.

How Do Mollusks Eat? Each type of mollusk has its own way of eating. Clams and other bivalves sit in one place and filter tiny plants, bacteria, and other particles from the water around them. Snails and slugs eat with a ribbonlike tongue covered with curved teeth, called a *radula* (RAJ oo luh). **Figure 16** shows a close-up of a slug's radula. Slugs and snails use the radula to scrape algae off rocks, chunks of tissue from seaweed, or pieces from the leaves of plants. Predatory snails and slugs often have large teeth on their radula that they use to attack their prey. And parasitic snails pierce their victims much as a mosquito does. Octopuses and squids use tentacles to grab their prey and place it in their powerful jaws, just as we can use our fingers to eat.

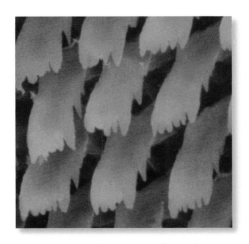

Figure 16 *The rows of teeth on a slug's radula help to scrape food from surfaces.*

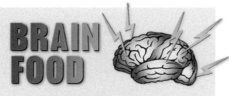
Have a Heart Unlike simpler invertebrates, mollusks have a circulatory system. Most mollusks have an **open circulatory system.** In this system, a simple heart pumps blood through blood vessels that empty into spaces in the animal's body called *sinuses.* This is very different from our own circulatory system, which is a **closed circulatory system.** In a closed circulatory system, a heart circulates blood through a network of blood vessels that form a closed loop. Cephalopods (squids and octopuses) also have a closed circulatory system, although it is much simpler than ours.

It's a Brain! Mollusks have complex ganglia. In most mollusks, these ganglia occur throughout the body. Mollusks have ganglia that control breathing, ganglia that move the foot, and ganglia that control digestion.

Cephalopods, like the one in **Figure 17,** have a more complex nervous system than the other mollusks have. In fact, octopuses and squids have the most advanced nervous system of all invertebrates. They have a brain, where all of their ganglia are connected. Not surprisingly, these animals are the smartest of all invertebrates. Octopuses, for example, can learn to navigate a maze and can distinguish between different shapes and colors. If they are given bricks or stones, they will build a cave to hide in.

Figure 17 *An octopus has a large brain. The brain coordinates the movement of its eight long arms.*

SECTION REVIEW

1. What are the four main parts of a mollusk's body?

2. What is the difference between an open circulatory system and a closed circulatory system?

3. **Analyzing Relationships** What two features do cephalopods share with humans that other mollusks do not?

Annelid Worms

You have probably seen earthworms, like the one in **Figure 18.** Earthworms belong to the phylum Annelida. Annelid worms are often called segmented worms because their body has segments. **Segments** are identical, or almost identical, repeating body parts.

These worms are much more complex than flatworms and roundworms. Annelid worms have a coelom and a closed circulatory system. They also have a nervous system that includes ganglia in each segment and a brain in the head. A nerve cord connects the brain and the ganglia.

Kinds of Annelid Worms   The annelid worms include three classes: earthworms, bristle worms, and leeches. Annelid worms live in salt water, in fresh water, or on land. They may scavenge anything edible, or they may prey on other organisms as predators or as parasites.

More than Just Bait   Earthworms are the most common annelid worms. An earthworm has 100 to 175 segments, most of which are identical. Some segments are specialized for eating and reproduction. Earthworms eat soil. They break down organic matter in the soil and excrete wastes called *castings*. Castings provide nutrients that plants can use. Earthworms also improve the soil by burrowing tunnels, which allow air and water to reach deep into the soil.

Earthworms have stiff bristles on the outside of their body to help them move. The bristles hold one part of the worm in place while the other part pushes through the soil.

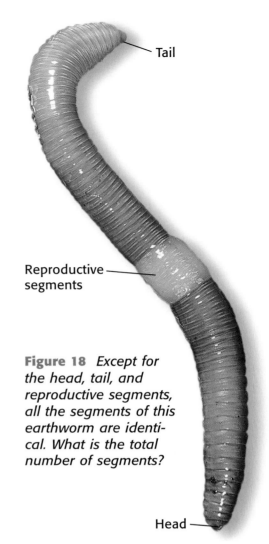

Tail

Reproductive segments

Head

Figure 18 *Except for the head, tail, and reproductive segments, all the segments of this earthworm are identical. What is the total number of segments?*

Do Worms Make Good Neighbors?

A friend of yours is worried because his garden is full of earthworms. He wants to find a way to get rid of the worms. Do you think this is a good idea? Why? Write a letter to your friend explaining what you think he should do.

Figure 19 *This bristle worm feeds by filtering particles from the water with its bristles. Can you see the segments on this worm?*

Bristles Can Be Beautiful If there were a beauty contest for worms, bristle worms would win. These remarkable worms come in many varieties and in brilliant colors. **Figure 19** shows a bristle worm. All bristle worms live in water. Some burrow through soggy sand and mud, eating whatever small creatures and particles they meet. Others crawl along the bottom, eating mollusks and other small animals.

Blood Suckers and More Leeches are known mostly as parasites that suck other animals' blood. This is true of some leeches, but not all. Other leeches are scavengers that eat dead animals. Still others are predators that prey on insects, slugs, and snails. Leeches that are parasites feed on the blood of other animals.

But leeches aren't all bad. Until the twentieth century, doctors regularly used leeches in medical treatments. Doctors attached leeches to a sick person to drain "bad" blood from the body. Although this practice is not accepted today, leeches are still used in medicine. After surgery, doctors sometimes use leeches to prevent dangerous swelling near a wound, as shown in **Figure 20.** Leeches also make a chemical that keeps blood from forming clots. Modern doctors give heart attack patients medicines that contain this chemical to keep blood clots from blocking arteries.

Figure 20 *Modern doctors sometimes use leeches to reduce swelling after surgery.*

internetconnect

SCI*LINKS*
NSTA

TOPIC: Mollusks and Annelid Worms
GO TO: www.scilinks.org
*sci*LINKS NUMBER: HSTL365

SECTION REVIEW

1. Name the three types of annelid worms. How are they alike? How are they different?

2. **Making Inferences** Why would a chemical that keeps blood from clotting be beneficial to leeches?

3. **Analyzing Relationships** How are annelid worms different from flatworms and roundworms? What characteristics do all worms share?

Terms to Learn

exoskeleton   mandible
compound eye   metamorphosis
antennae

What You'll Do

- List the four main characteristics of arthropods.
- Describe the different body parts of the four kinds of arthropods.
- Explain the two types of metamorphosis in insects.

Arthropods

Fiddler crab

They have lived here for hundreds of millions of years and have adapted to nearly all environments. An acre of land contains millions of them. You know them by more common names, such as insects, spiders, crabs, and centipedes. They are *arthropods,* the largest group of animals on Earth.

Seventy-five percent of all animal species are arthropods. The world population of humans is about 6 billion. Biologists estimate the world population of arthropods to be about a billion billion.

Characteristics of Arthropods

All arthropods share four characteristics: jointed limbs, a segmented body with specialized parts, an exoskeleton, and a well-developed nervous system.

Jointed Limbs Jointed limbs give arthropods their name. *Arthro* means "joint," and *pod* means "foot." Jointed limbs are arms, legs, or other similar body parts that bend at joints. Jointed limbs allow arthropods to move easily.

Segmented and Specialized Like annelid worms, arthropods are *segmented.* In some arthropods, such as the centipedes, nearly every segment is identical. Only the segments at the head and tail are different from the rest. Most other species of arthropods have segments that include very specialized parts, such as wings, antennae, gills, pincers, and claws. Many of these special parts form during the animal's development, when two or three segments grow together to form a *head,* a *thorax,* and an *abdomen.* These parts are labeled on the grasshopper pictured in **Figure 21.**

Mosquito

Tarantula

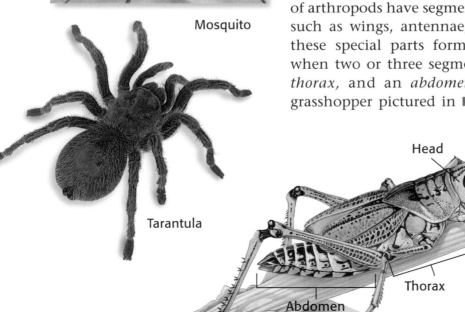

Head

Thorax

Abdomen

Figure 21 *The segments of this grasshopper fused together as the embryo grew to form a head, a thorax, and an abdomen.*

Invertebrates   **41**

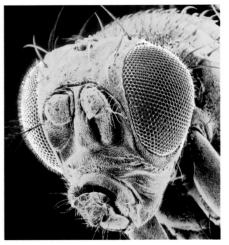

Figure 22 *Compound eyes consist of many individual light-sensitive cells that work together.*

Knights in Shining . . . Chitin? Arthropods have a hard **exoskeleton,** an external skeleton made of protein and a special substance called *chitin* (KIE tin). The exoskeleton does some of the same things an internal skeleton does. It provides a stiff frame that supports the animal's body. The exoskeleton also allows the animal to move. All of the muscles attach to different parts of the skeleton. When the muscles contract, they move the exoskeleton, which moves the parts of the animal.

But the exoskeleton also does things that internal skeletons don't do well. The exoskeleton acts like a suit of armor to protect internal organs and muscles. It also allows arthropods to live on land without drying out.

They've Got Smarts All arthropods have a head and a well-developed brain. The brain coordinates information from many sense organs, including eyes and bristles on the exoskeleton. Bristles sense movement, vibration, pressure, and chemicals. The eyes of some arthropods are very simple; they can detect light but cannot form an image. But most arthropods have compound eyes, which allow them to see images, although not as well as we do. A **compound eye** is made of many identical light-sensitive cells, as shown in **Figure 22.**

Kinds of Arthropods

Arthropods are classified according to the kinds of body parts they have. You can also tell the difference between arthropods by looking at the number of legs, eyes, and antennae they have. **Antennae** are feelers that respond to touch, taste, and smell.

Centipedes and Millipedes Centipedes and millipedes have a single pair of antennae, jaws called **mandibles,** and a hard *head capsule.* The easiest way to tell a centipede from a millipede is to count the number of legs per segment. Centipedes have one pair of legs per segment. Millipedes have two pairs of legs per segment. Take a look at **Figure 23.** How many legs can you count?

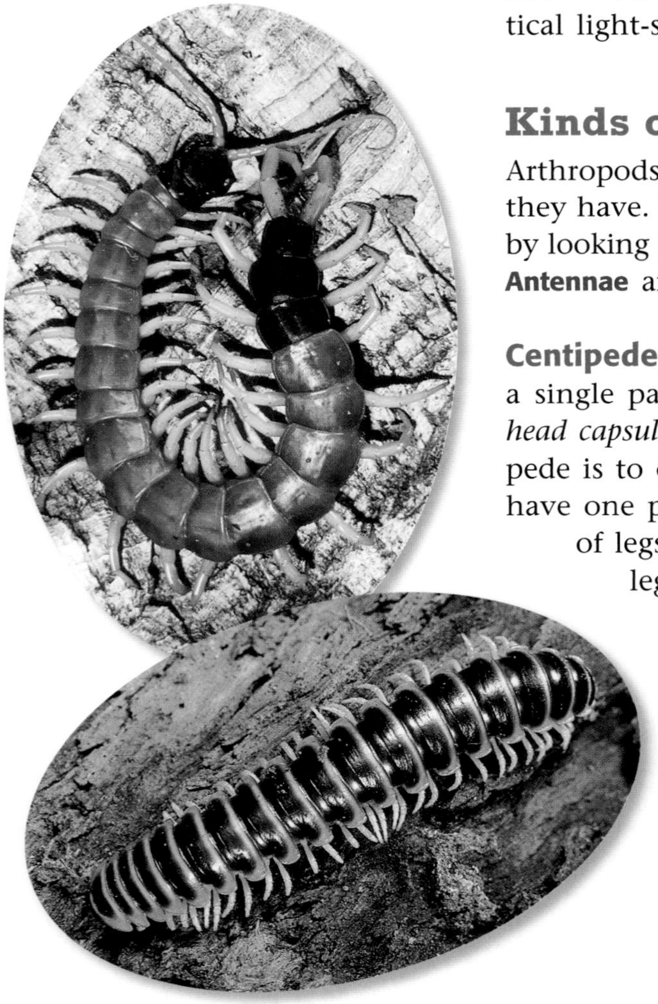

Figure 23 *Centipedes have one pair of legs per segment. The number of legs can range from 30 to 354. Millipedes have two pairs of legs per segment. The record number of legs on a millipede is 752!*

Crustaceans Crustaceans include shrimps, barnacles, crabs, and lobsters. Nearly all crustaceans are aquatic and have *gills* for breathing underwater. All crustaceans have mandibles and two pairs of antennae. Crustaceans have two compound eyes, usually on the end of stalks. The lobster in **Figure 24** shows all of these traits. The double antennae of crustaceans set them apart from all other arthropods.

Self-Check

What is the difference between a segmented worm and a centipede? *(See page 152 to check your answer.)*

Figure 24 *A lobster is a crustacean. It has compound eyes on the end of eye stalks.*

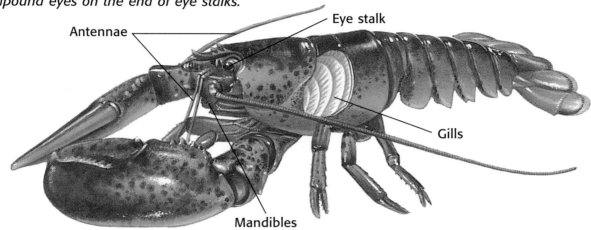

Eye stalk

Antennae

Gills

Mandibles

Arachnids Spiders, scorpions, mites, ticks, and daddy long-legs are all arachnids. **Figure 25** shows that an arachnid has two main body parts, the cephalothorax (SEF uh loh THOR AKS) and the abdomen. The *cephalothorax* consists of both a head and a thorax and usually has four pairs of walking legs. Arachnids have no antennae and no mandibles. Instead of mandibles, they have special mouthparts called *chelicerae* (kuh LIS uh ree), as illustrated in Figure 25. Some chelicerae look like pincers or fangs.

The eyes of arachnids are distinctive. While crustaceans and insects have compound eyes, arachnids do not. Spiders, for example, have eight simple eyes arranged in two rows at the front of the head. Count the eyes for yourself in **Figure 26.**

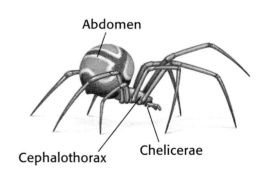

Abdomen

Cephalothorax

Chelicerae

Figure 25 *Arachnids have two main body parts and special mouthparts called chelicerae.*

Figure 26 *In addition to eight legs, spiders have eight eyes!*

Invertebrates **43**

Figure 27 American Dog Tick

Spiders and Ticks Spiders do not carry diseases and are enormously useful to humans. They kill more insect pests than any other animal, including birds. Several arachnids have painful bites or stings. But the fangs of small garden spiders cannot pierce human skin. In the United States, just three species of spiders—the black widow and two species of brown spider—have bites poisonous enough to kill a person. However, with proper medical treatment, they are not fatal.

Ticks live in forests, brushy areas, and even country lawns. **Figure 27** shows an American dog tick. Ticks that bite humans sometimes carry Lyme disease, Rocky Mountain spotted fever, and other diseases. Many people wear long pants and hats when going into areas where ticks live, and they check themselves for ticks after being outdoors. Fortunately, most people who are bitten by ticks do not get sick.

Insects The largest group of arthropods is insects. If you put all of the insects in the world together, they would weigh more than all other animals combined! **Figure 28** shows some of the wide variety of insects.

⏱️**Quick Lab**

Sticky Webs

Some spiders spin webs of sticky silk to trap their prey. Why don't spiders stick to their own webs? This experiment will show you the answer. Place a piece of **tape** on your desk sticky side up. The tape represents a web. Your fingers will represent an insect. Holding the tape in place by the edges, "walk" your fingers across the tape. What happens? Dip your fingers in **cooking oil,** and "walk" them across the tape again. What happens this time? Why? How might this experiment explain why spiders don't get stuck in their webs?

TRY at HOME

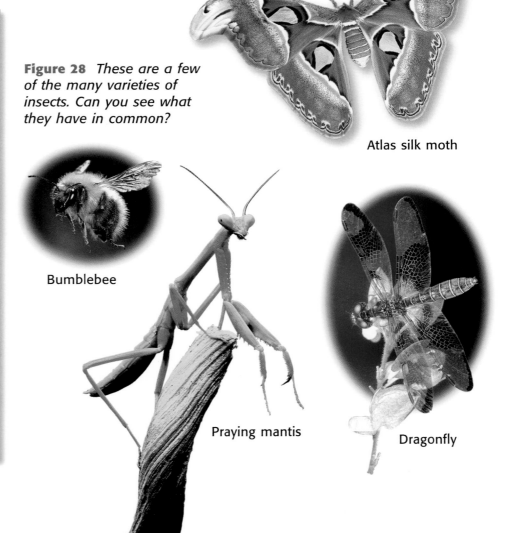

Figure 28 *These are a few of the many varieties of insects. Can you see what they have in common?*

Atlas silk moth

Bumblebee

Praying mantis

Dragonfly

Insects Are Everywhere (Almost) Insects live on land, in every freshwater environment, and at the edges of the sea. The only place on Earth insects do not live is in the ocean.

Many insects are beneficial. Most flowering plants depend on bees, butterflies, and other insects to carry pollen from one plant to another. Farmers depend on insects to pollinate hundreds of fruit crops, such as apples, cherries, tomatoes, and pumpkins.

Many insects are also pests. Fleas, lice, mosquitoes, and flies burrow into our flesh, suck our blood, or carry diseases. Plant-eating insects consume up to one-third of crops in this country, despite the application of pesticides.

Insect Bodies An insect's body has three parts: the head, the thorax, and the abdomen, as shown in **Figure 29.** On the head, insects have one pair of antennae and two compound eyes. They also have three pairs of mouthparts, including one pair of mandibles. The thorax is made of three segments, each with one pair of legs.

In many insects, the second and third segments of the thorax have a pair of wings. Some insects have no wings, and some have two pairs of wings.

Insect Development As an insect develops from an egg to an adult, it changes form. This process is called **metamorphosis.** There are two main types of metamorphosis, incomplete and complete. Primitive insects, such as grasshoppers and cockroaches, go through incomplete metamorphosis. In this metamorphosis there are only three stages: egg, nymph, and adult, as shown in **Figure 30.**

Figure 29 *Wasps have the same body parts as all other insects.*

Head

Thorax

Abdomen

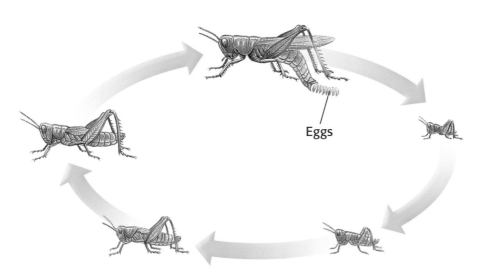

Eggs

Figure 30 *In incomplete metamorphosis, the larvae, called nymphs, look like smaller adults.*

Does a cricket like cold climates? Find out on page 126 of your LabBook.

Changing Form—Complete Metamorphosis

In complete metamorphosis, there are four stages: egg, larva, pupa, and adult. Butterflies, beetles, flies, bees, wasps, and ants go through this process. In complete metamorphosis, the larva looks very different from the adult.

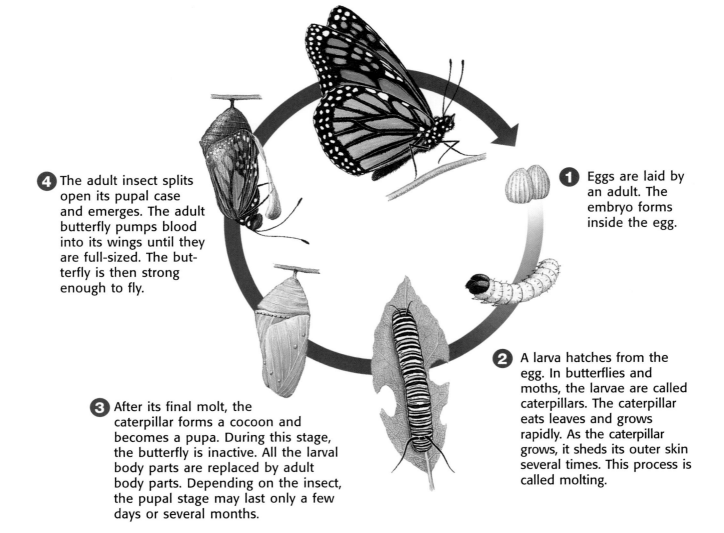

4 The adult insect splits open its pupal case and emerges. The adult butterfly pumps blood into its wings until they are full-sized. The butterfly is then strong enough to fly.

1 Eggs are laid by an adult. The embryo forms inside the egg.

3 After its final molt, the caterpillar forms a cocoon and becomes a pupa. During this stage, the butterfly is inactive. All the larval body parts are replaced by adult body parts. Depending on the insect, the pupal stage may last only a few days or several months.

2 A larva hatches from the egg. In butterflies and moths, the larvae are called caterpillars. The caterpillar eats leaves and grows rapidly. As the caterpillar grows, it sheds its outer skin several times. This process is called molting.

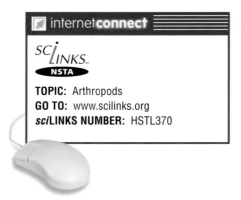

internetconnect

SCI LINKS
NSTA

TOPIC: Arthropods
GO TO: www.scilinks.org
sciLINKS NUMBER: HSTL370

SECTION REVIEW

1. Name the four kinds of arthropods. How are their bodies different?

2. What is the difference between complete metamorphosis and incomplete metamorphosis?

3. **Applying Concepts** Suppose you have found an arthropod in a swimming pool. The creature has compound eyes, antennae, and wings. Is it a crustacean? Why or why not?

Terms to Learn

endoskeleton
water vascular system

What You'll Do

◆ Describe three main characteristics of echinoderms.
◆ Describe the water vascular system.

Echinoderms

The last major phylum of invertebrates is Echinodermata. All echinoderms (ee KI noh DUHRMS) are marine animals. They include sea stars (starfish), sea urchins, sea lilies, sea cucumbers, brittle stars, and sand dollars. The smallest echinoderms are only a few millimeters across. The largest is a sea star that grows to 1 m in diameter.

Brittle star

Echinoderms live on the sea floor in all parts of the world's oceans. Some echinoderms prey on oysters and other shellfish, some are scavengers, and others scrape algae off rocky surfaces.

Sea star

Feather star

Spiny Skinned

The name *echinoderm* means "spiny skinned." The surface of the animal is not the spiny part, however. The body of the echinoderm contains an **endoskeleton,** an internal skeleton similar to the kind that vertebrates have. The hard, bony skeleton is usually covered with spines. The spines may be no more than sharp bumps, as in many sea stars. Or they may be long and pointed, as in sea urchins. All of the spines are covered by the outer skin of the animal.

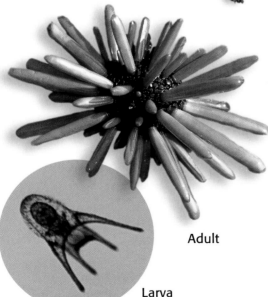

Adult

Larva

Bilateral or Radial?

Adult echinoderms have radial symmetry. But sea stars, sea urchins, sand dollars, and other echinoderms all develop from larvae with bilateral symmetry. **Figure 31** shows a sea urchin larva. Notice how the two sides are similar.

When echinoderm embryos first begin to develop, they form a mouth in the same way the embryos of vertebrates do. This is one of the reasons biologists think that vertebrates are more closely related to echinoderms than to other invertebrates.

Figure 31 *The sea urchin larva has bilateral symmetry. The adult sea urchin has radial symmetry.*

The Nervous System

All echinoderms have a simple nervous system similar to that of a jellyfish. Around the mouth is a circle of nerve fibers called the *nerve ring*. In sea stars, a *radial nerve* runs from the nerve ring to the tip of each arm, as shown in **Figure 32**. The radial nerves control the movements of the sea star's arms.

At the tip of each arm is a simple eye that senses light. The rest of the body is covered with cells that are sensitive to touch and to chemical signals in the water.

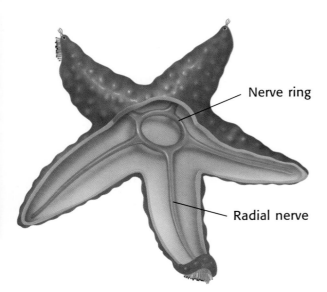

Figure 32 *Sea stars have simple nervous systems.*

Water Vascular System

One system that is unique to echinoderms is the **water vascular system.** This system uses water pumps to help the animal move, eat, breathe, and sense its environment. **Figure 33** shows the water vascular system of a sea star. Notice how water pressure from the water vascular system is used for a variety of functions.

Figure 33 *A water vascular system allows sea stars and all echinoderms to move, eat, and breathe.*

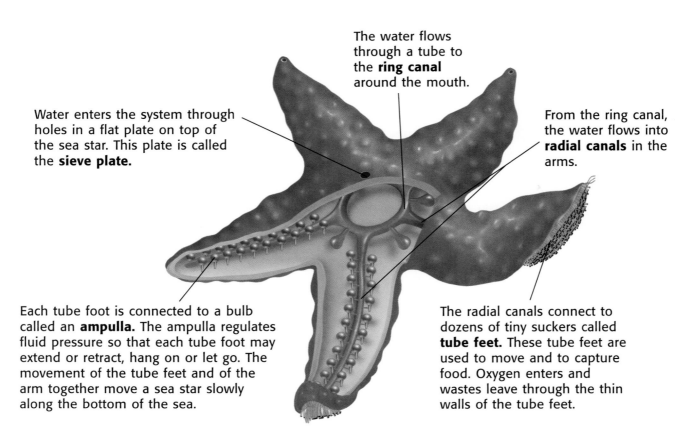

The water flows through a tube to the **ring canal** around the mouth.

Water enters the system through holes in a flat plate on top of the sea star. This plate is called the **sieve plate.**

From the ring canal, the water flows into **radial canals** in the arms.

Each tube foot is connected to a bulb called an **ampulla.** The ampulla regulates fluid pressure so that each tube foot may extend or retract, hang on or let go. The movement of the tube feet and of the arm together move a sea star slowly along the bottom of the sea.

The radial canals connect to dozens of tiny suckers called **tube feet.** These tube feet are used to move and to capture food. Oxygen enters and wastes leave through the thin walls of the tube feet.

Kinds of Echinoderms

Scientists divide echinoderms into several classes. Sea stars are the most familiar echinoderms, and they make up one class. But there are three classes of echinoderms that may not be as familiar to you.

Brittle Stars and Basket Stars The brittle stars and basket stars look like sea stars with long slender arms. These delicate creatures tend to be smaller than sea stars. **Figure 34** shows a basket star.

Sea Urchins and Sand Dollars Sea urchins and sand dollars are round, and their skeletons form a solid internal shell. They have no arms, but they use their tube feet to move in the same way as sea stars. Some sea urchins also walk on their spines. Sea urchins feed on algae they scrape from the surface of rocks and other objects and chew with special teeth. Sand dollars burrow into soft sand or mud, as shown in **Figure 35,** and eat tiny particles of food they find in the sand.

Sea Cucumbers Like sea urchins and sand dollars, sea cucumbers lack arms. A sea cucumber has a soft, leathery body. Unlike sea urchins, sea cucumbers are long and have a wormlike shape. **Figure 36** shows a sea cucumber.

Figure 34 *Basket stars have longer arms than sea stars.*

Figure 35 *Sand dollars burrow in the sand.*

Figure 36 *Like other echinoderms, sea cucumbers move with tube feet.*

SECTION REVIEW

1. How are sea cucumbers different from other echinoderms?

2. What is the path taken by water as it flows through the parts of the water vascular system?

3. **Applying Concepts** How are echinoderms different from other invertebrates?

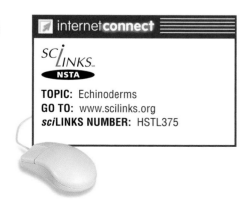

internet connect

SC*L*INKS
NSTA

TOPIC: Echinoderms
GO TO: www.scilinks.org
*sci*LINKS NUMBER: HSTL375

Skill Builder Lab

Porifera's Porosity

Early biologists thought that sponges were plants because sponges are like plants in some ways. In many species, the adults stick to a surface and stay there. They cannot chase their food. Sponges absorb and filter a lot of water to get food.

In this activity, you will observe the structure of a sponge. You will also think about how a sponge's structure affects its ability to hold water and catch food. You will think about how the size of the sponge's holes affects the amount of water the sponge can hold.

MATERIALS

- natural sponge
- kitchen sponge
- paper towel
- balance
- bowl (large enough for sponge and water)
- water
- graduated cylinder
- funnel
- calculator (optional)

Make Observations

1 Put on your safety goggles and lab apron. Observe the natural sponge. Identify the pores on the outside of the sponge. See if you can find the central cavity and oscula. Record your data in your ScienceLog.

2 Notice the size and shape of the holes. Look at the holes in the kitchen sponge and the holes in the paper towel. How do their holes compare with the sponge's natural holes?

Form a Hypothesis

3 Which item do you think can hold the most water per gram of dry mass? Formulate a testable hypothesis and record it in your ScienceLog.

Test the Hypothesis

4 Read steps 5–9. Using a computer or your ScienceLog, design and draw a data table. Remember, you will collect data for the natural sponge, the kitchen sponge, and the paper towel.

5 Use the balance to measure the mass of your sponge. Record the mass.

6 Place the sponge in the bowl. Use the graduated cylinder to add water to the sponge. Add 10 mL at a time until the sponge is completely soaked. Record the amount of water added.

7 Gently remove the sponge from the bowl. Use the funnel and the graduated cylinder to measure the amount of water left in the bowl. How much water did the sponge absorb? Record your data.

8 Calculate how many milliliters of water your sponge holds per gram of dry sponge. For example, if your sponge's dry mass is 12 g and your sponge holds 59.1 mL of water, then your sponge holds 4.9 mL of water per gram.

$$\left(\frac{59.1 \text{ mL}}{12 \text{ g}} = 4.9 \text{ mL/g}\right)$$

9 Repeat steps 5–8 using the kitchen sponge and the paper towel.

Analyze the Results

10 Which item held the most water per gram of dry mass?

11 Did your results support your hypothesis?

12 Do you see a connection between the size of an item's holes and the item's ability to hold water?

Draw Conclusions

13 What can you conclude about how the size and shape of a sponge's holes affect the feeding ability of a sponge?

Going Further

You have just studied how a sponge's body structure complements its feeding function. Now collect a few different types of live insects. Using good animal safety, observe how they eat and examine the structure of their mouthparts. How does the structure of their mouthparts complement the mouthparts' function? Record your answers in your ScienceLog.

Chapter Highlights

SECTION 1

Vocabulary

invertebrate (*p. 28*)

bilateral symmetry (*p. 28*)

radial symmetry (*p. 28*)

asymmetrical (*p. 28*)

ganglia (*p. 29*)

gut (*p. 29*)

coelom (*p. 29*)

Section Notes

- Invertebrates are animals without a backbone.

- Most animals have radial symmetry or bilateral symmetry.

- Unlike other animals, sponges have no symmetry.

- A coelom is a space inside the body. The gut hangs inside the coelom.

- Ganglia are clumps of nerves that help control the parts of the body.

- Sponges have special cells called collar cells to digest their food.

- Cnidarians have special stinging cells to catch their prey.

- Cnidarians have two body forms, the polyp and the medusa.

- Tapeworms and flukes are parasitic flatworms.

SECTION 2

Vocabulary

open circulatory system (*p. 38*)

closed circulatory system (*p. 38*)

segment (*p. 39*)

Section Notes

- All mollusks have a foot, a visceral mass, and a mantle. Most mollusks also have a shell.

- Mollusks and annelid worms have both a coelom and a circulatory system.

- In an open circulatory system, the heart pumps blood through vessels into spaces called sinuses. In a closed circulatory system, the blood is pumped through a closed network of vessels.

- Segments are identical or nearly identical repeating body parts.

☑ Skills Check

Math Concepts

SPEED AND DISTANCE If a snail is moving at 30 cm/h, how far can it travel in 1 minute? There are 60 minutes in 1 hour:

$$\frac{30 \text{ cm}}{60 \text{ min}} = 0.5 \text{ cm/min}$$

In 1 minute the snail will travel 0.5 cm.

Visual Understanding

METAMORPHOSIS Some insects go through incomplete metamorphosis, and some go through complete metamorphosis. Look at the illustrations on pages 45 and 46 to see the difference between these two types of metamorphosis.

SECTION 3

Vocabulary

exoskeleton *(p. 42)*

compound eye *(p. 42)*

antennae *(p. 42)*

mandible *(p. 42)*

metamorphosis *(p. 45)*

Section Notes

- Seventy-five percent of all animals are arthropods.

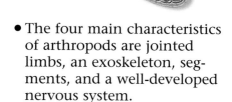

- The four main characteristics of arthropods are jointed limbs, an exoskeleton, segments, and a well-developed nervous system.

- Arthropods are classified by the type of body parts they have.

- The four kinds of arthropods are centipedes and millipedes, crustaceans, arachnids, and insects.

- Insects can undergo complete or incomplete metamorphosis.

Labs

The Cricket Caper *(p. 126)*

SECTION 4

Vocabulary

endoskeleton *(p. 47)*

water vascular system *(p. 48)*

Section Notes

- Echinoderms are marine animals that have an endoskeleton and a water vascular system.

- Most echinoderms have bilateral symmetry as larvae and radial symmetry as adults.

- The water vascular system allows echinoderms to move around by means of tube feet, which act like suction cups.

- Echinoderms have a simple nervous system consisting of a nerve ring and radial nerves.

🔲 internet connect

GO TO: go.hrw.com

Visit the **HRW** Web site for a variety of learning tools related to this chapter. Just type in the keyword:

KEYWORD: HSTINV

GO TO: www.scilinks.org

Visit the **National Science Teachers Association** on-line Web site for Internet resources related to this chapter. Just type in the **sci**LINKS number for more information about the topic:

TOPIC: Sponges	**sci**LINKS NUMBER: HSTL355
TOPIC: Roundworms	**sci**LINKS NUMBER: HSTL360
TOPIC: Mollusks and Annelid Worms	**sci**LINKS NUMBER: HSTL365
TOPIC: Arthropods	**sci**LINKS NUMBER: HSTL370
TOPIC: Echinoderms	**sci**LINKS NUMBER: HSTL375

Chapter Review

To complete the following sentences, choose the correct term from each pair of terms listed below:

1. Animals without a backbone are called ___?___. (*invertebrates* or *vertebrates*)

2. A sponge uses ___?___ to pull water in and releases water out through ___?___. (*an osculum* or *pores*)

3. Cnidarians have ___?___ symmetry and flatworms have ___?___ symmetry. (*radial* or *bilateral*)

4. The shell of a snail is secreted by the ___?___. (*radula* or *mantle*)

5. Annelid worms have ___?___. (*jointed limbs* or *segments*)

6. An ampulla regulates ___?___. (*water pressure in a tube foot* or *blood pressure in a closed circulatory system*)

UNDERSTANDING CONCEPTS

Multiple Choice

7. Invertebrates make up what percentage of all animals?
   a. 4 percent
   b. 50 percent
   c. 85 percent
   d. 97 percent

8. Which of the following describes the body plan of a sponge:
   a. radial symmetry
   b. bilateral symmetry
   c. asymmetry
   d. partial symmetry

9. What cells do sponges have that no other animal has?
   a. blood cells
   b. nerve cells
   c. collar cells
   d. none of the above

10. Which of the following animals do not have ganglia?
    a. annelid worms
    b. cnidarians
    c. flatworms
    d. mollusks

11. Which of the following animals has a coelom?
    a. sponge
    b. cnidarian
    c. flatworm
    d. mollusk

12. Both tapeworms and leeches are
    a. annelid worms.
    b. parasites.
    c. flatworms.
    d. predators.

13. Some arthropods do not have
    a. jointed limbs.
    b. an exoskeleton.
    c. antennae.
    d. segments.

14. Echinoderms live
    a. on land.
    b. in fresh water.
    c. in salt water.
    d. All of the above

15. *Echinoderm* means
    a. "jointed limbs."
    b. "spiny skinned."
    c. "endoskeleton."
    d. "shiny tube foot."

16. Echinoderm larvae have
    a. radial symmetry.
    b. bilateral symmetry.
    c. no symmetry.
    d. radial and bilateral symmetry.

Short Answer

17. What is a gut?

18. How are arachnids different from insects?

19. Which animal phylum contains the most species?

20. How does an echinoderm move?

Concept Mapping

21. Use the following terms to create a concept map: insect, sponges, sea anemone, invertebrates, arachnid, sea cucumber, crustacean, centipede, cnidarians, arthropods, echinoderms.

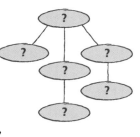

Write one or two sentences to answer the following questions:

22. You have discovered a strange new animal that has bilateral symmetry, a coelom, and nerves. Will this animal be classified in the Cnidaria phylum? Why or why not?

23. Unlike other mollusks, cephalopods can move rapidly. Based on what you know about the body parts of mollusks, why do you think cephalopods have this ability?

24. Roundworms, flatworms, and annelid worms belong to different phyla. Why aren't all the worms grouped in the same phylum?

MATH IN SCIENCE

25. If 75 percent of all animals are arthropods and 40 percent of all arthropods are beetles, what percentage of all animals are beetles?

INTERPRETING GRAPHICS

Below is an evolutionary tree showing how the different phyla of animals may be related to one another. The "trunk" of the tree is on the left. Use the tree to answer the questions that follow.

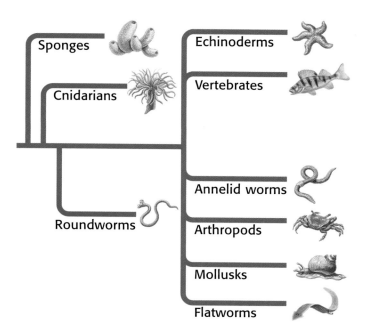

26. Which phylum is the oldest?

27. Are mollusks more closely related to roundworms or flatworms?

28. What phylum is most closely related to the vertebrates?

Reading Check-up

Take a minute to review your answers to the Pre-Reading Questions found at the bottom of page 26. Have your answers changed? If necessary, revise your answers based on what you have learned since you began this chapter.

WATER BEARS

You're alive and you know it, but how? Well, eating, breathing, and moving around are all pretty sure signs of life. And once something stops eating or breathing, the end is near. Or is it? Oddly enough, this doesn't seem to be the case for one group of invertebrates–the water bears.

Grin and Bear It

When conditions get really rough—too hot, too cold, but mostly too dry to survive—a water bear will shut down its body processes. It's similar to a bear going into hiberna-tion, but it is even more extreme. When a water bear can't find water, it dries itself out and forms a sugar that coats its cells. Scientists think this may keep the water bear's cells from breaking down, and it may be the key to its survival.

Water Bear

During this hibernation-like state, called *cryptobiosis* (CRIP toh bie OH sis), the water bear doesn't eat, move, or breathe. And amazingly, it doesn't die either. Once you add water, the water bear will come right back to normal life!

Hard to Put a Finger On

Officially called tardigrades (TAHR di graydz), water bears have been difficult to classify. But the 700 different species of water bears are probably most closely related to arthropods. Most make their homes on wet mosses and lichens. Some water bears feed on nematodes (a tiny, unsegmented worm) and rotifers (a tiny wormlike or spherical animal). Most feed on the fluids from mosses found near their homes.

From the tropics to the Arctic, the world is full of water bears. None are much larger than a grain of sand, but all have a slow, stomping walk. Some tardi-grades live as deep as the bottom of the ocean, more than 4,700 m below sea level. Other water bears live at eleva-tions of 6,600 m above sea level, well above the tree line. It is a wonder how water bears can withstand the range of temperatures found in these places, from 151°C to −270°C.

On Your Own

▶ What do you think people can learn from an organism like the water bear? Write down at least one reason why it is worthwhile to study these special creatures.

EYE ON THE ENVIRONMENT

Sizable Squid

"Before my eyes was a horrible monster . . . It swam crossways in the direction of the *Nautilus* with great speed, watching us with its enormous staring green eyes. The monster's mouth, a horned beak like a parrot's, opened and shut vertically." So wrote Jules Verne in his science-fiction story *Twenty Thousand Leagues Under the Sea.* But what was this horrible monster that was about to attack the submarine *Nautilus*? Believe it or not, it was a creature that actually exists—a giant squid!

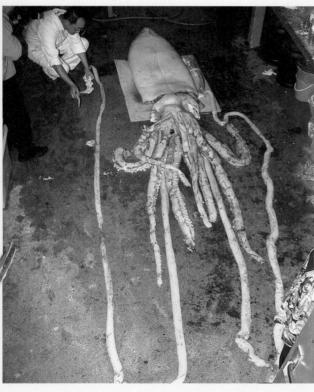

▲ *This giant squid was already dead when it was caught in a fishing net off the coast of New Zealand.*

Squid Facts

As the largest of all invertebrates, giant squids range from 8 m to 25 m long and weigh as much as 2,000 kg. It's hard to know for sure, though, because no one has ever studied a living giant squid. Scientists have studied only dead or dying giant squids that have washed ashore or have been trapped in fishing nets.

Giant squids are very similar to their much smaller relatives. They have a torpedo-shaped body, two tentacles, eight arms, a mantle, a funnel, and a beak. All their body parts are much larger, though! A giant squid's eyes, for instance, may be as large as a volleyball! And like adult squids of smaller species, giant squids feed not only on fish but also on smaller squids. Given the size of giant squids, it's hard to imagine that they have any enemies in the ocean, but they do.

A Hungry Enemy

Weighing in at 20 tons, toothed sperm whales eat giant squids. How do we know this? As many as 10,000 squid beaks have been found in the stomach of a single sperm whale. The hard beaks of giant squids are indigestible. It seems that giant squids are a regular meal for sperm whales. Yet this meal can result in some battle scars. Many whales bear ring marks on their forehead and fins that match the size of the suckers found on giant squids.

Fact or Fiction?

▶ Read Chapter 18 of Jules Verne's *Twenty Thousand Leagues Under the Sea,* and then try to find other stories about squids. Write your own story about a giant squid, and share it with the class.

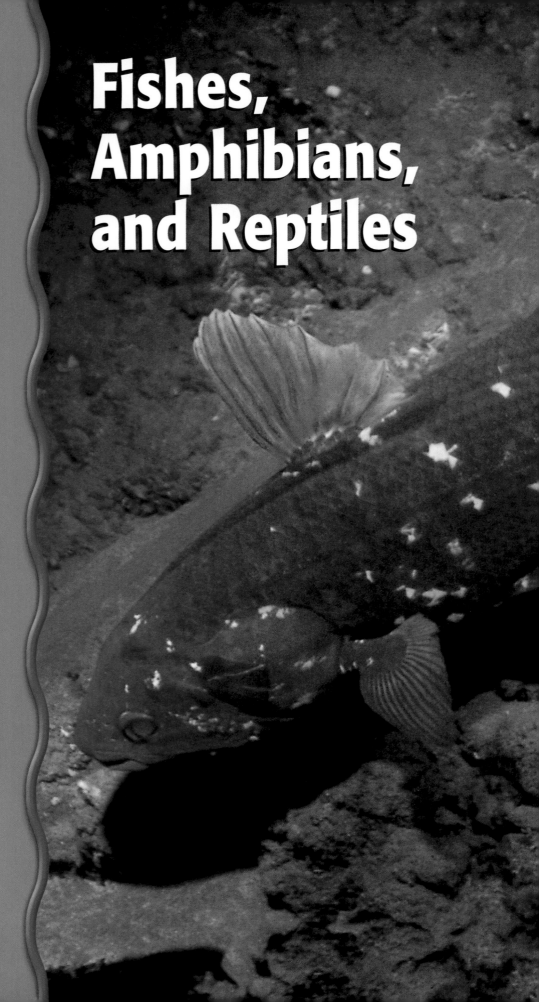

Fishes, Amphibians, and Reptiles

Pre-Reading Questions

1. What does it mean to say an animal is cold–blooded?

2. What is the difference between a reptile and an amphibian?

A BLAST FROM THE PAST!

In December 1938, Marjorie Courtenay Latimer made an amazing discovery. On a fishing dock in South Africa, she found a coelacanth (SEE luh kahnth). She sent a sketch of the fish to her friend J.L.B. Smith, an expert on fish. Smith recognized the fish right away. So what's so amazing about this giant fish? Scientists had thought that coelacanths became extinct about 70 million years ago! In this chapter, you will learn about other fishes as well as about amphibians and reptiles.

OIL ON WATER

To stay afloat, sharks store a lot of oil in their liver. In this activity, you will build a model of an oily liver to see how an oily liver can keep a shark afloat.

Procedure

1. Use a **beaker** to measure out equal amounts of **water** and **cooking oil.**

2. Fill **one balloon** with the water.

3. Fill a **second balloon** with the cooking oil.

4. Tie the balloons so that no air remains inside. Float each balloon in a **bowl half full of water.** Observe what happens to the balloons.

Analysis

5. Compare how the two balloons floated.

6. The function of an oily liver is to keep the fish from sinking. How does the structure of the liver complement its function?

What You'll Do

◆ List the four characteristics of chordates.
◆ Describe the main characteristics of vertebrates.
◆ Explain the difference between an ectotherm and an endotherm.

What Are Vertebrates?

Have you ever seen a dinosaur skeleton at a museum? Fossilized dinosaur bones were put back together to show what the animal looked like. Most dinosaur skeletons are huge compared with the skeletons of the humans who view them. But humans have many of the same kinds of bones that dinosaurs had; ours are just smaller. Your backbone is very much like the one in a dinosaur skeleton, as shown in **Figure 1.** Animals with a backbone are called **vertebrates.**

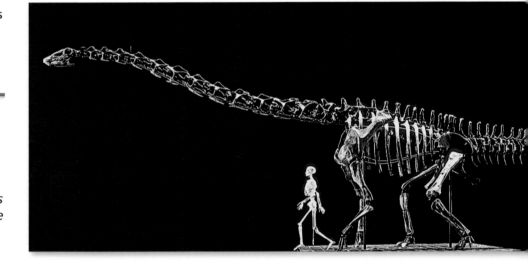

Figure 1 *Humans and dinosaurs are both vertebrates.*

Chordates

Vertebrates belong to the phylum Chordata. Members of this phylum are called *chordates*. Vertebrates make up the largest group of chordates, but there are two other groups of chordates—lancelets and tunicates. These are shown in **Figure 2.** These chordates do not have a backbone or a well-developed head. They are very simple compared with vertebrates. But all three groups share chordate characteristics.

At some point in their life, all chordates have four special body parts: a *notochord,* a *hollow nerve cord, pharyngeal* (fuh RIN jee uhl) *pouches,* and a *tail.* These are shown in **Figure 3** on the next page.

Figure 2 *Both tunicates, like the sea squirts at left, and the lancelet, shown above, are marine organisms.*

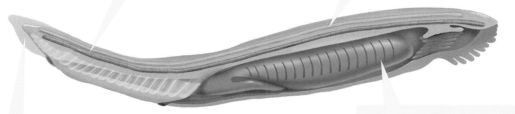

A stiff but flexible rod called a **notochord** gives the body support. In most vertebrates, the embryo's notochord disappears and a backbone grows in its place.

A **hollow nerve cord** runs along the back and is full of fluid. In vertebrates, this nerve cord is called the *spinal cord,* and it is filled with *spinal fluid.*

Chordates have a **tail** that begins behind the anus. Some chordates have a tail in only the embryo stage.

Pharyngeal pouches are found in all chordate embryos. These develop into gills or other body parts as the embryo matures.

Figure 3 *The chordate characteristics in a lancelet are shown here. All chordates have these four characteristics at some point in their life.*

Getting a Backbone

Most chordates are vertebrates. Vertebrates have many traits that set them apart from the lancelets and tunicates. For example, vertebrates have a backbone. The backbone is a segmented column of bones. These bones are called **vertebrae** (VUHR tuh BRAY). You can see the vertebrae of a human in **Figure 4.** The vertebrae surround the nerve cord and protect it. Vertebrates also have a well-developed head protected by a skull. The skull and vertebrae are made of either cartilage or bone. *Cartilage* is the tough material that the flexible parts of our ears and nose are made of.

The skeletons of all vertebrate embryos are made of cartilage. But as most vertebrates grow, the cartilage is usually replaced by bone. Bone is much harder than cartilage.

Because bone is so hard, it can easily be fossilized. Many fossils of vertebrates have been discovered, and they have provided valuable information about relationships among organisms.

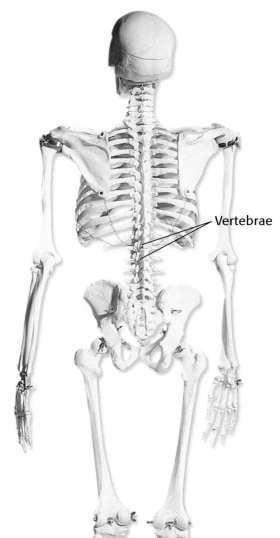

Vertebrae

Figure 4 *The vertebrae interlock to form a strong but flexible column of bone. The backbone protects the spinal cord and supports the rest of the body.*

Are Vertebrates Warm or Cold?

Most animals need to stay warm. The chemical reactions that take place in their body cells occur only at certain tempera-tures. An animal's body temperature cannot be too high or too low. But some animals control their body temperature more than others.

Staying Warm   Birds and mammals warm their body by capturing the heat released by the chemical reactions in their cells. Their body temperature stays nearly constant even as the temperature of their environment changes. Animals that main-tain a constant body temperature are called **endotherms.** Endotherms are sometimes called *warmblooded* animals. Because of their constant body temperature, endotherms can live in cold environments.

Cold Blood?   On sunny days, lizards, like the one in **Figure 5,** bask in the sun. As they become warm, they also become more active. They are able to hunt for food and escape predators. But when the temperature drops, lizards slow down.

Lizards and other animals that do not control their body temperature through the chemical reactions of their cells are called **ectotherms.** Their body temperature fluctuates with the temperature of their environment. Nearly all fishes, amphibians, and reptiles are ectotherms. Ectotherms are sometimes called *coldblooded* animals.

Figure 5 *Lizards bask in the sun to absorb heat.*

SECTION REVIEW

1. How are vertebrates the same as other chordates? How are they different?

2. How are endotherms and ectotherms different?

3. **Applying Concepts**   Your pet lizard is not moving very much. The veterinarian tells you to put a heat lamp in the cage. Why might this help?

Terms to Learn

fins   gills
scales   denticles
lateral line   swim bladder
   system

What You'll Do

◆ Describe the three classes of living fishes, and give an example of each.

◆ Describe the function of a swim bladder and an oily liver.

◆ Explain the difference between internal fertilization and external fertilization.

Fishes

Find a body of water, and you'll probably find fish. Fishes live in almost every water environment, from shallow ponds and streams to the depths of the oceans. You can find fishes in cold arctic waters and in warm tropical seas. Fishes can be found in rivers, lakes, marshes, and even in water-filled caves.

Fish were the first vertebrates on Earth. Fossil evidence indicates that fish appeared about 500 million years ago. Today Earth's marine and freshwater fishes make up more species than all other vertebrates combined. There are more than 25,000 species of fishes, and more are being discovered. A few are shown in **Figure 6.**

Angelfish

Figure 6 *These are just some of the many species of fishes. Do any look familiar?*

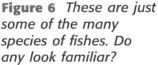
Catfish

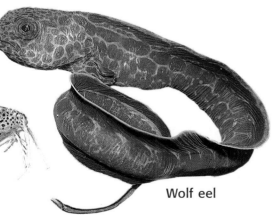
Wolf eel

Surgeonfish

Sea horse

Fish Characteristics

Although the fishes on this page look very different from each other, they share many characteristics that help them live in water.

Many fishes are predators of other animals. Others are herbivores. Because they must actively search for food, they need a strong body, well-developed senses, and a brain.

Born to Swim Fishes have many body parts that help them swim. Strong muscles attached to the backbone allow fishes to swim vigorously after their prey. Fishes swim through the water by moving their fins. **Fins** are fanlike structures that help fish move, steer, stop, and balance. Many fishes have bodies covered by **scales,** which protect the body and reduce friction as they swim through the water. **Figure 7** shows some of the external features of a typical fish.

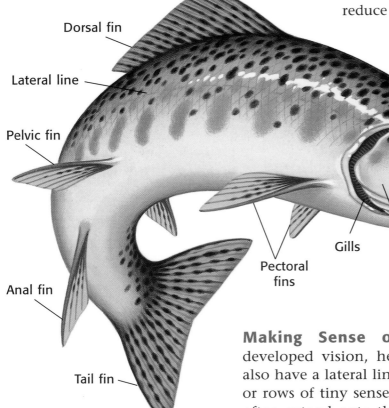

Dorsal fin

Lateral line

Pelvic fin

Anal fin

Tail fin

Pectoral fins

Gills

Gill cover

Eye

Figure 7 Fishes come in a variety of shapes and sizes, but all have gills, fins, and a tail.

Making Sense of the World Fishes have well-developed vision, hearing, and sense of smell. Most fishes also have a lateral line system. The **lateral line system** is a row or rows of tiny sense organs along each side of the body that often extend onto the head. This system detects water vibrations, such as those caused by another fish swimming by. Fishes have a brain that keeps track of all the information coming in from these senses. A tough skull protects the brain.

Underwater Breathing Fishes breathe with gills. **Gills** are organs that remove oxygen from the water. Oxygen in the water passes through the thin membrane of the gills to the blood. The blood then carries oxygen throughout the body. Gills are also used to remove carbon dioxide from the blood.

Making More Fish Most fishes reproduce by *external fertilization.* The female lays unfertilized eggs in the water, and the male drops sperm on them. But some species of fish reproduce by internal fertilization. In *internal fertilization,* the male deposits sperm inside the female. In most cases the female then lays eggs that contain the developing embryos. Baby fish hatch from the eggs. But in some species, the embryos develop inside the mother, and the baby fish are born live.

Physics
C O N N E C T I O N

When you look at an object through a magnifying glass, you have to move the lens back and forth in front of your eye to bring the object into focus. The same thing happens in fish eyes. Fish have special muscles to change the position of the lenses of their eyes. By moving the eye lenses, fish can bring objects into focus.

Types of Fishes

Fishes include five very different classes of animals. Two classes are now extinct. We know about them only because of fossils. The three classes of fishes living today are *jawless fishes, cartilaginous fishes,* and *bony fishes.*

Jawless Fishes The first fishes did not have jaws. You might think that having no jaws would make it hard to eat and would lead to extinction. But the jawless fishes have thrived for half a billion years. Today there are about 60 species of jawless fishes.

Modern jawless fishes include lampreys, as shown in **Figure 8,** and hagfish. These fishes are eel-like, and they have smooth, slimy skin and a round, jawless mouth. Their skeleton is made of cartilage, and they have a notochord but no backbone. These fishes have a skull, a brain, and eyes.

Figure 8 *Lampreys are parasites that live by attaching themselves to other fishes.*

Cartilaginous Fishes Did you know that a shark is a fish? Sharks, like the one in **Figure 9,** belong to a class of fishes called cartilaginous (KART'l AJ uh nuhs) fishes. In most vertebrates, soft cartilage in the embryo is gradually replaced by bone. In sharks, skates, and rays, however, the skeleton never changes from cartilage to bone. That is why they are called cartilaginous fishes.

Figure 9 *Sharks, like this hammerhead, rarely prey on humans. They prefer to eat their regular food, which is fish.*

Sharks are the most well-known cartilaginous fishes, but they are not the only ones. Another group includes skates and rays. A sting ray is shown in **Figure 10.**

As any shark lover knows, cartilaginous fishes have fully functional jaws. These fishes are strong swimmers and expert predators. Like most predators, they have keen senses. Many have excellent senses of sight and smell, and they have a lateral line system.

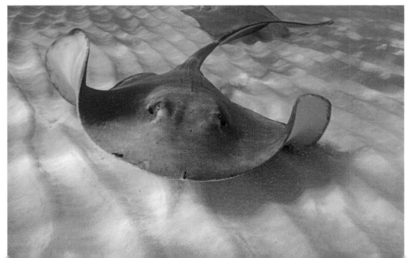

Figure 10 *Rays, like this sting ray, usually feed on shellfish and worms on the sea floor.*

Fishes, Amphibians, and Reptiles **65**

Figure 11 *A shark's denticles and human teeth are made of the same materials.*

The skin of cartilaginous fishes is covered with small tooth-like **denticles** that give it the feel of sandpaper. If you rub your hand on a shark's skin from head to tail, it feels smooth. But if you rub your hand from tail to head, you can get cut! Look at the magnified denticles in **Figure 11.**

To stay afloat, cartilaginous fishes store a lot of oil in their liver. Even with oily livers, these fishes are heavier than water. They have to keep moving in order to stay afloat. Once they stop swimming, they gradually glide to the bottom.

Cartilaginous fishes do not swim just to keep from sinking, however. Some must swim to maintain the flow of water over their gills. If these fishes stop swimming, they will suffocate. Others do not have to swim. They can lie on the ocean floor and pump water across their gills.

Bony Fishes When you think of a fish, you probably think of something like the fish shown in **Figure 12.** Goldfish, tuna, trout, catfish, and cod are all bony fishes, the largest class of fishes. Ninety-five percent of all fishes are bony fishes. They range in size from 1 cm long to more than 6 m long.

As their name implies, bony fishes have a skeleton made of bone instead of cartilage. The body of a bony fish is covered by bony scales.

Unlike cartilaginous fishes, bony fishes can float in one place without swimming. This is because they have a swim bladder that keeps them from sinking. The **swim bladder** is a balloonlike organ that is filled with oxygen and other gases from the bloodstream. It gives fish *buoyancy*, or the ability to float in water. The swim bladder and other body parts of bony fishes are shown in **Figure 13.**

Figure 12 *A goldfish is a bony fish.*

MATH **BREAK**

A Lot of Bones

If there are 25,000 species of fishes and 95 percent of all fishes are bony fishes, how many species of bony fishes are there?

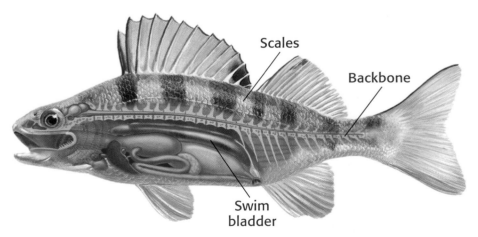

Figure 13 *Bony fishes have a swim bladder, a bony skeleton, and scales.*

Scales

Backbone

Swim bladder

There are two main groups of bony fishes. Almost all bony fishes are *ray-finned fishes*. Ray-finned fishes have paired fins supported by thin rays of bone. Ray-finned fishes include many familiar fishes, such as eels, herrings, trout, minnows, and perch. **Figure 14** shows a ray-finned fish.

Lobe-finned fishes and *lungfishes* make up a second group of bony fishes. Lobe-finned fishes have fins that are muscular and thick. There are six known species of modern lungfishes. You can see a lungfish in **Figure 15.** Scientists think that ancient fishes from this group were the ancestors of amphibians.

Figure 14 *Ray-finned fishes are some of the fastest swimmers in the world. A pike, like this one, can swim as fast as the fastest human runners can run, about 48 km/h.*

Figure 15 *Lungfishes have air sacs, or lungs, and can gulp air. They are found in Africa, Australia, and South America and live in shallow waters that often dry up in the summer.*

SECTION REVIEW

1. What are the three types of fishes? Which type are the coelacanths?

2. Most bony fishes reproduce by external fertilization. What does this mean?

3. What is the lateral line system, and what is its function?

4. **Analyzing Relationships** Compare the ways that cartilaginous fishes and bony fishes maintain buoyancy.

Fishes, Amphibians, and Reptiles   **67**

SECTION 3

Terms to Learn

lung   metamorphosis
tadpole

What You'll Do

◆ Describe the importance of amphibians in evolution.
◆ Explain how amphibians breathe.
◆ Describe metamorphosis in amphibians.

Amphibians

By the end of the Devonian period, 350 million years ago, fishes lived wherever there was water. But none of these vertebrates could live on land. And the land was a wonderful place for a vertebrate. It had lush green forests, many tasty insects, and few predators. But for vertebrates to adapt to life on land, they needed lungs for breathing and legs for walking. How did these changes occur?

Moving to Land

Most of the amphibians living on Earth today are frogs or salamanders, like those in **Figure 16.** But the early amphibians looked much different. Fossil evidence indicates that the first amphibians evolved from ancient ancestors of modern lungfishes. These fishes developed lungs to get oxygen from the air. A **lung** is a saclike organ that takes oxygen from the air and delivers it to the blood. The fins of these ancient fishes became strong enough to support the fishes' body weight and eventually became legs.

Fossils show that the first amphibians looked like a cross between a fish and a salamander, as shown in **Figure 17.** The early amphibians were the first vertebrates to live most of their life on land, and they were very successful. Many were very large—up to 10 m long—and could stay on dry land longer than today's amphibians can. But early amphibians still had to return to the water to keep from drying out, to avoid overheating, and to lay their eggs.

Figure 16 *Modern amphibians include frogs and salamanders.*

Barred leaf frog

Sierra Nevada salamander

Figure 17 *Ancient amphibians probably looked something like this.*

Characteristics of Amphibians

Amphibian means "double life." Most amphibians have two parts to their life. Because amphibian eggs do not have a shell and a special membrane to prevent water loss, the embryos must develop in a very wet environment. After amphibians emerge from an egg, they live in the water, like fishes do. Later they develop into animals that can live on land. But even adult amphibians are only partly adapted to life on land, and they must always live near water.

Amphibians are ectotherms. Like the body of a fish, the body of an amphibian changes temperature according to the temperature of its environment.

Thin-Skinned Most amphibians do not have scales. Their skin is thin, smooth, and moist. They do not drink water. Instead, they absorb it through their skin. Amphibians can breathe by gulping air into their lungs. But many also absorb oxygen through their skin, which is full of blood vessels. Some salamanders, like the one in **Figure 18,** breathe only through their skin. Because amphibian skin is so thin and moist, these animals can lose water through their skin and become dehydrated. For this reason, most amphibians live in water or in damp habitats.

The skin of many amphibians is brilliantly colored. The colors are often a warning to predators because the skin of many amphibians contains poison glands. These poisons may simply be irritating or they may be deadly. The skin of the dart-poison frog, shown in **Figure 19,** contains one of the most deadly toxins known.

Figure 18 *The four-toed salamander has no lungs. It gets all of its oxygen through its skin.*

Figure 19 *The skin of this dart-poison frog is full of poison glands. In South America, hunters rub the tips of their arrows in the deadly toxin.*

Self-Check

How is amphibian skin like a lung? *(See page 152 to check your answers.)*

Fishes, Amphibians, and Reptiles **69**

Leading a Double Life The amphibian embryo usually develops into an aquatic larva called a **tadpole.** The tadpole can live only in wet environments. It obtains oxygen through gills and uses its long tail to swim. Later the tadpole loses its gills and develops lungs and limbs. This change from a larval form to an adult form is called **metamorphosis** and is shown in **Figure 20.** Adult amphibians are capable of surviving on land.

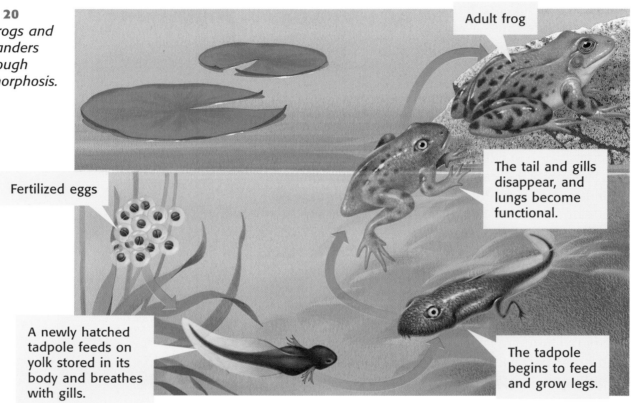

Figure 20
Most frogs and salamanders go through metamorphosis.

Adult frog

The tail and gills disappear, and lungs become functional.

Fertilized eggs

A newly hatched tadpole feeds on yolk stored in its body and breathes with gills.

The tadpole begins to feed and grow legs.

A few amphibians skip the aquatic stage and develop directly into adult frogs or salamanders. For example, one species of frog lays eggs on moist ground. Male adults guard the developing embryos. When an embryo begins to move, a male frog quickly takes it into its mouth and protects it inside its vocal sacs. When the embryo finishes developing, the adult frog opens its mouth, and a tiny frog jumps out. You can see this frog in **Figure 21.**

Figure 21 *Darwin frogs live in Chile and Argentina. A male frog may carry 5 to 15 embryos in its vocal sacs until the young are about 1.5 cm in length.*

Kinds of Amphibians

It is estimated that there are 4,600 species of amphibians alive today. These belong to three groups: caecilians (see SIL yuhns), salamanders, and frogs and toads.

Caecilians Most people are not familiar with caecilians. These amphibians do not have legs and are shaped like worms or snakes, as shown in **Figure 22.** But they have the thin, moist skin of amphibians. Unlike other amphibians, some caecilians have bony scales. Many caecilians have very small eyes underneath their skin and are blind. Caecilians live in the tropical areas of Asia, Africa, and South America. About 160 species are known.

Figure 22 *Caecilians are legless amphibians that live in damp soil in the tropics. Caecilians eat small invertebrates in the soil.*

Salamanders Of modern amphibians, salamanders are the most like prehistoric amphibians. Although salamanders are much smaller than their ancient ancestors, they have a similar body shape, a long tail, and four strong legs. They range in size from a few centimeters long to 1.5 m long.

There are about 390 known species of salamanders. Most of them live under stones and logs in the damp woods of North America. They eat small invertebrates. A few, such as the axolotl (AK suh LAHT 'l), shown in **Figure 23,** do not go through metamorphosis. They live their entire life in the water.

Figure 23 *This axolotl is an unusual salamander. It retains its gills and never leaves the water.*

APPLY

Ecological Indicators

Amphibians are often called ecological indicators. When large numbers of amphibians begin to die or show deformities, this may indicate a problem with the environment.

Sometimes deformities are caused by parasites, but amphibians are also extremely sensitive to chemical changes in their environment. Based on what you know about amphibians, why do you think they are sensitive to water pollution and air pollution?

Frogs and Toads Ninety percent of all amphibians are frogs or toads. They are found all over the world, from deserts to rain forests. Frogs and toads are very similar to each other, as you can see in **Figure 24.** In fact, toads are a type of frog.

Frog

Toad

Figure 24 *Frogs have smooth, moist skin. Toads spend less time in water than frogs do, and their skin is drier and bumpier.*

Frogs and toads are highly adapted for life on land. Adults have powerful leg muscles for jumping. They have well-developed ears for hearing, and they have vocal cords for calling. They also have extendible, sticky tongues. The tongue is attached to the front of the mouth so that it can be flipped out quickly to catch insects.

Singing Frogs Frogs are well known for their nighttime choruses, but many frogs sing in the daytime too. Like humans, they force air from their lungs across vocal cords in the throat. But frogs have something we lack. Surrounding their vocal cords is a thin sac of skin called the *vocal sac.* When frogs vocalize, the sac inflates with air, like a balloon does, and vibrates. You can see this in **Figure 25.** The vibrations of the sac increase the volume of the song so that it can be heard over long distances.

Figure 25 *Most frogs that sing are males, and their songs have different meanings.*

Examine the princely characteristics of a friendly frog on page 128 of your LabBook.

SECTION REVIEW

1. Describe metamorphosis in amphibians.

2. Why do amphibians have to be near water or in a very wet habitat?

3. What adaptations allow amphibians to live on land?

4. Name the three types of amphibians. How are they similar? How are they different?

5. **Analyzing Relationships** Describe the relationship between lungfishes and amphibians. What characteristics do they share? How do they differ?

Terms to Learn

therapsid
amniotic egg

What You'll Do

◆ Explain the adaptations that allow reptiles to live on land.
◆ Name the three main groups of vertebrates that evolved from reptiles.
◆ Describe the characteristics of an amniotic egg.
◆ Name the three orders of modern reptiles.

Reptiles

About 35 million years after the first amphibians colonized the land, some of them evolved special traits that prepared them for life in an even drier environment. These animals developed thick, dry skin that protected them from water loss. Their legs became stronger and more vertical, so they were better able to walk. And they evolved a special egg that could be laid on dry land. These animals were reptiles, the first animals to live completely out of the water.

Reptile History

Fossils show that soon after the first reptiles appeared, they split into groups. This can be shown in a family tree of the reptiles, as illustrated in **Figure 26.**

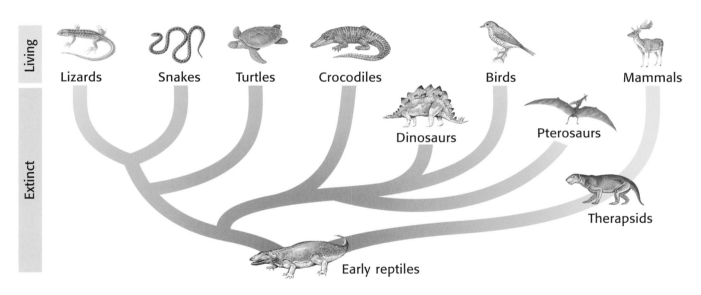

Figure 26 *Early reptiles were the ancestors of modern reptiles, birds, and mammals.*

Many of the most fascinating reptiles are now extinct. When we think of extinct reptiles, we usually think of dinosaurs. But only a fraction of the reptiles living in prehistoric times were land-dwelling dinosaurs. Many were swimming reptiles. A few were flying pterosaurs. And there were turtles, lizards, snakes, and crocodiles. In addition, there was a group of mammal-like reptiles called therapsids. As you can see in Figure 26, **therapsids** (thuh RAP sidz) were the ancestors of mammals.

Characteristics of Reptiles

Reptiles are adapted for life on land. Although crocodiles, turtles, and a few species of snakes live in the water, all of these animals are descended from reptiles that lived on land. All reptiles use lungs to breathe air, just as you do.

Thick-Skinned A very important adaptation for life on land is thick, dry skin, which forms a watertight layer. This thick skin keeps cells from losing water by evaporation. Most reptiles cannot breathe through their skin the way amphibians can. Most depend entirely on their lungs for oxygen and carbon dioxide exchange. Check out the snake's skin in **Figure 27.**

Coldblooded? Like fishes and amphibians, reptiles are ectotherms. That means that they usually cannot maintain a constant body temperature. Reptiles are active when their environment is warm, and they slow down when their environment is cool.

A few reptiles can generate some heat from their own body. For example, some lizards in the southwestern United States can keep their body temperature at about 34°C, even when the air temperature is cool. Still, modern reptiles are limited to mild climates. They cannot tolerate the cold polar regions, where many mammals and birds thrive.

The Amazing Amniotic Egg Among reptiles' many adaptations to land life, the most critical is the amniotic (AM nee AH tik) egg. The **amniotic egg** is surrounded by a shell, as shown in **Figure 28.** The shell protects the developing embryo and keeps the egg from drying out. An amniotic egg can be laid under rocks, in the ground, in forests, or even in the desert. The amniotic egg is so well adapted to a dry environment that even crocodiles and turtles return to land to lay their eggs.

Figure 27 *Many people think snakes are slimy, but the skin of snakes and other reptiles is scaly and dry.*

Figure 28 *Compare the amphibian eggs at left with the reptile eggs at right. What differences can you see?*

Parts of an Amniotic Egg The shell is just one important part of an amniotic egg. The other parts of an amniotic egg are illustrated in **Figure 29.** The egg protects the developing embryo from predators, bacterial infections, and dehydration.

Figure 29 An Amniotic Egg

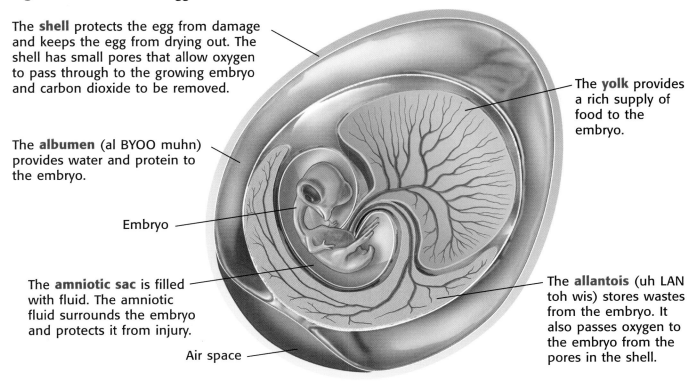

The **shell** protects the egg from damage and keeps the egg from drying out. The shell has small pores that allow oxygen to pass through to the growing embryo and carbon dioxide to be removed.

The **albumen** (al BYOO muhn) provides water and protein to the embryo.

Embryo

The **amniotic sac** is filled with fluid. The amniotic fluid surrounds the embryo and protects it from injury.

Air space

The **yolk** provides a rich supply of food to the embryo.

The **allantois** (uh LAN toh wis) stores wastes from the embryo. It also passes oxygen to the embryo from the pores in the shell.

Reptile Reproduction The amniotic egg is fertilized inside the female. A shell then forms around the egg, and the female lays the egg. Because of the shell, reptiles can reproduce only by internal fertilization.

Most reptiles lay their eggs in soil or sand. A few do not lay eggs. Instead the embryos develop inside the mother's reproductive passages, and the young are born live. In either case, the embryo develops into a tiny young reptile. Reptiles do not have a larval stage and do not undergo metamorphosis.

Types of Reptiles

In the age of the dinosaurs, from 300 million years ago until about 65 million years ago, most land vertebrates were reptiles. Today the 6,000 species of living reptiles represent only a handful of the many species of reptiles that once lived.

Modern reptiles include turtles and tortoises, crocodiles and alligators, and lizards and snakes.

Self-Check

1. What adaptations of reptiles are important for living on dry land?

2. Why must animals that lay eggs with shells reproduce by internal fertilization?

(See page 152 to check your answers.)

Figure 30 *The bottom shell of a box turtle is hinged on both ends so the turtle can pull it snug against the top shell.*

Turtles and Tortoises The 250 species of turtles and tortoises are only distantly related to the rest of the reptiles.

The trait that makes turtles and tortoises unique is their shell. The shell makes a turtle slow and inflexible, so outrunning its predators is highly unlikely. On the other hand, many turtles can draw their head and limbs into the armorlike shell to protect themselves, as the box turtle shown in **Figure 30** is doing.

Most turtles spend some or all of their life in water. The front legs of sea turtles have evolved into flippers, as shown in **Figure 31**. Female sea turtles come ashore only to lay their eggs on sandy beaches. Desert tortoises are different from other turtles. They live only on land.

Figure 31 *Sea turtles have a streamlined shell to help them swim and turn rapidly.*

Crocodiles and Alligators The 22 species of crocodiles and alligators are all carnivores. They eat water bugs, fish, turtles, birds, and mammals. These reptiles spend most of their time in the water. Because their eyes and nostrils are on the top of their flat head, they can watch their surroundings while most of their body is hidden underwater. This gives them a great advantage over their prey. How can you tell the difference between an alligator and a crocodile? See for yourself in **Figure 32.**

Figure 32 *An alligator has a broad head and a rounded snout. A crocodile has a narrow head and a pointed snout.*

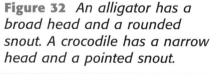

Lizards Most of the species of modern reptiles are lizards and snakes. There are about 4,000 known species of lizards and about 1,600 known species of snakes.

Lizards live in deserts, forests, grasslands, and jungles. Chameleons, geckos, skinks, and iguanas are some of the amazing variety of lizards. Most lizards eat small invertebrates, but many are herbivores. The largest lizard is the 3 m long, 140 kg Komodo dragon of Indonesia, shown in **Figure 33.** But most lizards are less than 30 cm long.

Figure 33 *Komodo dragons eat deer, pigs, and goats. They have even been known to eat humans in rare cases.*

Snakes The most obvious characteristic of snakes is their lack of legs. Snakes move by contractions of their muscular body. On smooth surfaces, scales on their belly grip the surface and help pull the snake forward.

All snakes are carnivores. They eat small animals and eggs. Snakes swallow their prey whole, as shown in **Figure 34.** Snakes have special jaws with five joints that allow them to open their mouth wide and swallow very large prey. Some snakes, such as pythons and boas, kill their prey by squeezing it until it suffocates. Other snakes have poison glands and special fangs for injecting venom into their prey. The venom kills or stuns the prey and contains powerful enzymes that begin digesting it.

Snakes do not see or hear well, but they can smell extremely well. When a snake flicks its forked tongue out of its mouth, it is sampling the air. Tiny particles and molecules stick to the tongue. When the snake pulls its tongue inside its mouth, it places the tips of its tongue into two openings in the roof of its mouth, where the molecules are sensed.

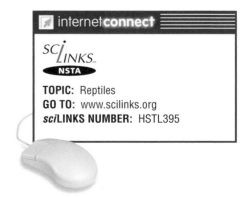

Figure 34 *This common egg eater snake is swallowing a bird's egg.*

SECTION REVIEW

1. What characteristics set turtles apart from other reptiles?

2. What special adaptations do snakes have for eating?

3. **Applying Concepts** Like reptiles, mammals have an amniotic egg. But mammals give birth to live young. The embryo develops from a fertilized egg inside the female's body. Which parts of a reptilian amniotic egg do you think a mammal could do without? Explain your answer.

internet**connect**

SC*LINKS*
NSTA

TOPIC: Reptiles
GO TO: www.scilinks.org
*sci*LINKS NUMBER: HSTL395

Making Models Lab

Floating a Pipe Fish

Bony fishes control how deep or shallow they swim with an organ called a swim bladder. As gases are absorbed and released by the swim bladder, the fish rises or sinks in the water. In this activity, you will make a model of a fish with a swim bladder. Your challenge will be to make the fish float halfway between the top of the water and the bottom of the container. It will probably take several tries and a lot of observing and analyzing along the way.

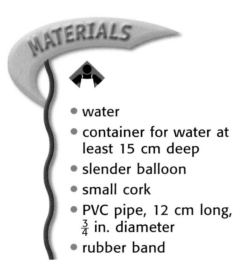

MATERIALS

- water
- container for water at least 15 cm deep
- slender balloon
- small cork
- PVC pipe, 12 cm long, $\frac{3}{4}$ in. diameter
- rubber band

Make a Prediction

1. Estimate how much air you will need in the balloon so that your pipe fish will float halfway between the top of the water and the bottom of the container. Will you need to inflate the balloon halfway, just a small amount, or all the way? The balloon will have to fit inside the pipe, but there will need to be enough air to make the pipe float. Write your prediction in your ScienceLog.

Build a Model

2. Inflate your balloon. Hold the neck of the balloon so that no air escapes, and push the cork into the end of the balloon. If the cork is properly placed, no air should leak out when the balloon is held under water.

3. Place your swim bladder inside the pipe, and place a rubber band along the pipe as shown. The rubber band will keep the swim bladder from coming out of either end.

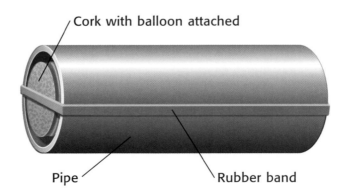

Cork with balloon attached

Pipe

Rubber band

Collect Data

4 Place your pipe fish in the water, and note where the fish floats. Record your observations in your ScienceLog.

5 If the pipe fish does not float where you want, take it out of the water, adjust the amount of air in the balloon, and try again.

6 You can release small amounts of air from the bladder by carefully lifting the neck of the balloon away from the cork. You can add more air by removing the cork and blowing more air into the balloon. Keep adjusting and testing until your fish floats halfway between the bottom of the container and the top of the water.

Analyze the Results

7 Was the estimate you made in step 1 correct? Explain your answer.

8 In relation to the length and volume of the entire pipe fish, how much air was needed to make the fish float? State your answer as a percentage.

9 Based on the amount of space the balloon took up in your model, how much space do you estimate is taken up by a swim bladder inside a living fish? Explain.

10 What are some limitations to your model?

Going Further
Some fast-swimming fishes, such as sharks, and marine mammals, such as whales and dolphins, do not have a swim bladder. Find out from the library or the Internet how these animals keep from sinking to the bottom of the ocean. Create a poster, and explain your results on index cards. Include drawings of the fish or marine mammals you have researched.

Chapter Highlights

Vocabulary

vertebrate *(p. 60)*

vertebrae *(p. 61)*

endotherm *(p. 62)*

ectotherm *(p. 62)*

Section Notes

- At some point during their development, chordates have a notochord, a hollow nerve cord, pharyngeal pouches, and a tail.

- Chordates include lancelets, tunicates, and vertebrates. Most chordates are vertebrates.

- Vertebrates differ from the other chordates in that they have a backbone and skull made of bone or cartilage.

- The backbone is composed of units called vertebrae.

- Vertebrates may be ectotherms or endotherms.

- Endotherms control their body temperature through the chemical reactions of their cells. Ectotherms do not.

Vocabulary

fins *(p. 64)*

scales *(p. 64)*

lateral line system *(p. 64)*

gills *(p. 64)*

denticles *(p. 66)*

swim bladder *(p. 66)*

Section Notes

- There are three groups of living fishes: jawless fishes, cartilaginous fishes, and bony fishes.

- The cartilaginous fishes have an oily liver that helps them float.

☑ Skills Check

Math Concepts

HOW MANY SPECIES? If there are 6,000 species of reptiles and 67 percent of all reptiles are lizards, how many species of lizards are there?

Sixty-seven percent of 6,000 is:

$$6{,}000 \times 0.67 = 4{,}020$$

There are 4,020 species of lizards.

Visual Understanding

METAMORPHOSIS Most amphibians go through metamorphosis. They change form as they develop into an adult. Figure 20 on page 70 illustrates the metamorphosis of a frog. Follow the arrows to see how a frog develops from an egg to a tadpole to an adult.

SECTION 2

- Most bony fishes have a swim bladder. The swim bladder is a balloonlike organ that gives bony fishes buoyancy.

- In external fertilization, eggs are fertilized outside the female's body. In internal fertilization, eggs are fertilized inside the female's body.

SECTION 3

Vocabulary

lung *(p. 68)*

tadpole *(p. 70)*

metamorphosis *(p. 70)*

Section Notes

- Amphibians were the first vertebrates to live on land.

- Amphibians breathe by gulping air into their lungs and by absorbing oxygen through their skin.

- Amphibians start life in water, where they breathe through gills. During metamorphosis, they lose their gills and develop lungs and legs that allow them to live on land.

- Modern amphibians include caecilians, salamanders, and frogs and toads.

Labs

A Prince of a Frog *(p. 128)*

SECTION 4

Vocabulary

therapsid *(p. 73)*

amniotic egg *(p. 74)*

Section Notes

- Reptiles evolved from amphibians by adapting to life on dry land.

- Reptiles have thick, scaly skin that protects them from drying out.

- A tough shell keeps the amniotic egg from drying out and protects the embryo.

- Amniotic fluid surrounds and protects the embryo in an amniotic egg.

- Vertebrates that evolved from early reptiles are reptiles, birds, and mammals.

- Modern reptiles include turtles and tortoises, lizards and snakes, and crocodiles and alligators.

---

 internetconnect

GO TO: go.hrw.com

Visit the **HRW** Web site for a variety of learning tools related to this chapter. Just type in the keyword:

KEYWORD: HSTVR1

 **N S T A**

GO TO: www.scilinks.org

Visit the **National Science Teachers Association** on-line Web site for Internet resources related to this chapter. Just type in the *sci*LINKS number for more information about the topic:

TOPIC:	sciLINKS NUMBER:
TOPIC: Vertebrates	*sci***LINKS NUMBER:** HSTL380
TOPIC: Fishes	*sci***LINKS NUMBER:** HSTL385
TOPIC: Amphibians	*sci***LINKS NUMBER:** HSTL390
TOPIC: Reptiles	*sci***LINKS NUMBER:** HSTL395

Chapter Review

USING VOCABULARY

To complete the following sentences, choose the correct term from each pair of terms listed below:

1. At some point in their development, all chordates have __?__. *(lungs and a notochord* or *a hollow nerve cord and a tail)*

2. Mammals evolved from early ancestors called __?__. *(therapsids* or *dinosaurs)*

3. Fish are __?__. *(endotherms* or *ectotherms)*

4. When a frog lays eggs that are later fertilized by sperm, it is an example of __?__ fertilization. *(internal* or *external)*

5. The vertebrae wrap around and protect the __?__ of vertebrates. *(notochord* or *hollow nerve cord)*

UNDERSTANDING CONCEPTS

Multiple Choice

6. Which of the following is not a vertebrate?
   a. tadpole
   b. lizard
   c. lamprey
   d. tunicate

7. Tadpoles change into frogs by the process of
   a. evolution.
   b. internal fertilization.
   c. metamorphosis.
   d. temperature regulation.

8. The swim bladder is found in
   a. jawless fishes.
   b. cartilaginous fishes.
   c. bony fishes.
   d. lancelets.

9. The amniotic egg first evolved in
   a. bony fishes.
   b. birds.
   c. reptiles.
   d. mammals.

10. The yolk holds
    a. food for the embryo.
    b. amniotic fluid.
    c. wastes.
    d. oxygen.

11. Both bony fishes and cartilaginous fishes have
    a. denticles.
    b. fins.
    c. an oily liver.
    d. a swim bladder.

12. Reptiles are adapted to a life on land because
    a. they can breathe through their skin.
    b. they are ectotherms.
    c. they have thick, moist skin.
    d. they have an amniotic egg.

Short Answer

13. How do amphibians breathe?

14. What characteristics allow fish to live in the water?

15. How does an embryo in an amniotic egg get oxygen?

Concept Mapping

16. Use the following terms to create a concept map: dinosaur, turtle, reptiles, amphibians, fishes, shark, salamander, vertebrates.

CRITICAL THINKING AND PROBLEM SOLVING

Write one or two sentences to answer the following questions:

17. Suppose you have found an animal that has a backbone and gills, but you can't find a notochord. Is it a chordate? How can you be sure?

18. Suppose you have found a shark that lacks the muscles needed to pump water over its gills. What does that tell you about the shark's lifestyle?

19. A rattlesnake does not see very well, but it can detect a temperature change of as little as three-thousandths of a degree Celsius. How is this ability useful to a rattlesnake?

20. It's 43°C outside, and the normal body temperature of a velociraptor is 38°C. Would you most likely find the raptor in the sun or in the shade? Explain.

MATH IN SCIENCE

21. A Costa Rican viper can eat a mouse that has one-third more mass than the viper. How much can you eat? Write down your mass in kilograms. To find your mass in kilograms, divide your mass in pounds by 2.2. If you were to eat a meal with a mass one-third larger than your mass, what would the mass of the meal be in kilograms?

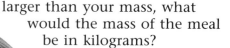

INTERPRETING GRAPHICS

Examine the graph of body temperatures below, and answer the questions that follow.

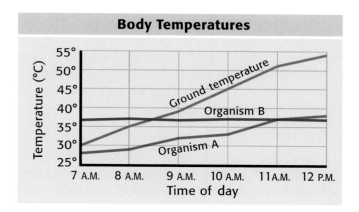

Body Temperatures

22. How do the body temperatures of organism A and organism B change with the ground temperature?

23. Which of these organisms is most likely an ectotherm? Why?

24. Which of these organisms is most likely an endotherm? Why?

Reading Check-up

Take a minute to review your answers to the Pre-Reading Questions found at the bottom of page 58. Have your answers changed? If necessary, revise your answers based on what you have learned since you began this chapter.

Robot Fish

When is a fish tail not a fish tail? When it's the tail of RoboTuna, a robotic fish designed by scientists at the Massachusetts Institute of Technology.

Something Fishy Going On

There's no doubt about it—fish are quicker and much more maneuverable than most ships and submarines. So why aren't ships and submarines built more like fish—with tails that flap back and forth? This question caught the imagination of some scientists at MIT and inspired them to build RoboTuna, a model of a bluefin tuna. This robot fish is 124 cm long and is composed of six motors, a skin of foam and Lycra™, and a skeleton of aluminum ribs and hinges connected by pulleys and strings.

A Tail of Force and Motion

The MIT scientists propose that if ships were designed to more closely resemble fish, the ships would use much less energy and thus save money. A ship moving through water leaves a trail of little whirlpools called *vortices*

behind it. These vortices increase the friction between the ship and the water. A fish, however, senses the vortices and responds by flapping its tail, creating vortices of its own. The fish's vortices counteract the effects of the original vortices, and the fish is propelled forward with much less effort.

RoboTuna has special sensors that measure changes in water pressure in much the same way that a living tuna senses vortices. Then the robot fish flaps its vortex-producing tail, allowing it to swim like a living fish. As strange as it may seem, RoboTuna may represent the beginning of a new era in nautical design.

Viewing Vortices

▶ Fill a roasting pan three-quarters full with water. Wait long enough for the water to stop moving. Then tie a 6 cm piece of yarn or ribbon to the end of a pencil. Drag the pencil through the water with the yarn or ribbon trailing behind it. How does the yarn or ribbon respond? Where are the vortices?

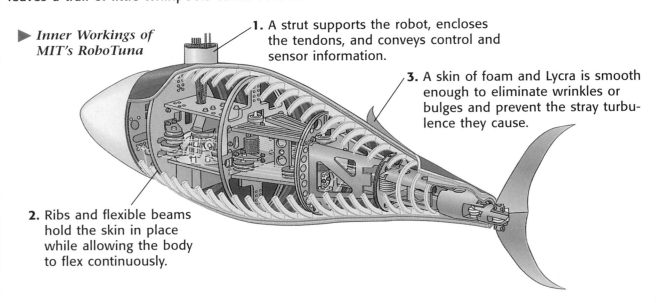

▶ *Inner Workings of MIT's RoboTuna*

1. A strut supports the robot, encloses the tendons, and conveys control and sensor information.

3. A skin of foam and Lycra is smooth enough to eliminate wrinkles or bulges and prevent the stray turbulence they cause.

2. Ribs and flexible beams hold the skin in place while allowing the body to flex continuously.

WARM BRAINS IN COLD WATER

Of the world's 30,000 kinds of fish, only a few carry around their own brain heaters. *Brain heaters?* Why would a fish need a special heater just for its brain? Before you can answer that question, you have to think about how fish keep warm in the cold water of the ocean.

A Question of Temperature

Most fish and marine organisms are ectotherms. An ectotherm's body temperature closely matches the temperature of its surroundings. Endotherms, on the other hand, maintain a steady body temperature regardless of the temperature of their surroundings. Humans are endotherms. Other mammals, such as dogs, elephants, whales, and birds, are also endotherms. But only a few kinds of fish—tuna, for example—are endotherms. These fish are still coldblooded, but they can heat certain parts of their bodies. Endothermic fish can hunt for prey in extremely chilly water. Yet these fish pay a high price for their ability to inhabit very cold areas—they use a lot of energy.

Being endothermic requires far more energy than being ectothermic. Some fish, such as swordfish, marlin, and sailfish, have adaptations that let them heat only part of their body. Instead of using large amounts of energy to warm the entire body, they warm only their eyes and brain. That's right—they have special brain heaters!

▶ *Why do you think it is important to protect the brain and eyes from extreme cold?*

Warming the Brain

In a "brain-warming" fish, a small mass of muscle attached to each eye acts as a thermostat. It adjusts the temperature of the brain and eyes as the fish swims through different temperature zones. These "heater muscles" help maintain delicate nerve functions that are important to finding prey.

Heater muscles allow the swordfish, for example, to swim in both warm surface waters of the ocean and depths of 485 m, where the temperature drops to near freezing. This adaptation has an obvious advantage: It gives the fish a large range of places to look for food.

Ectotherms in Action

▶ Contact a local pet store that sells various kinds of fish. Find out what water temperature is best for different fish from different regions of the Earth. For example, compare the ideal water temperatures for goldfish, discus fish, and angelfish. Why do you think fish-tank temperatures must be carefully controlled?

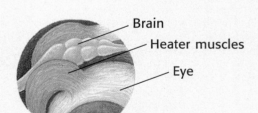

Brain
Heater muscles
Eye

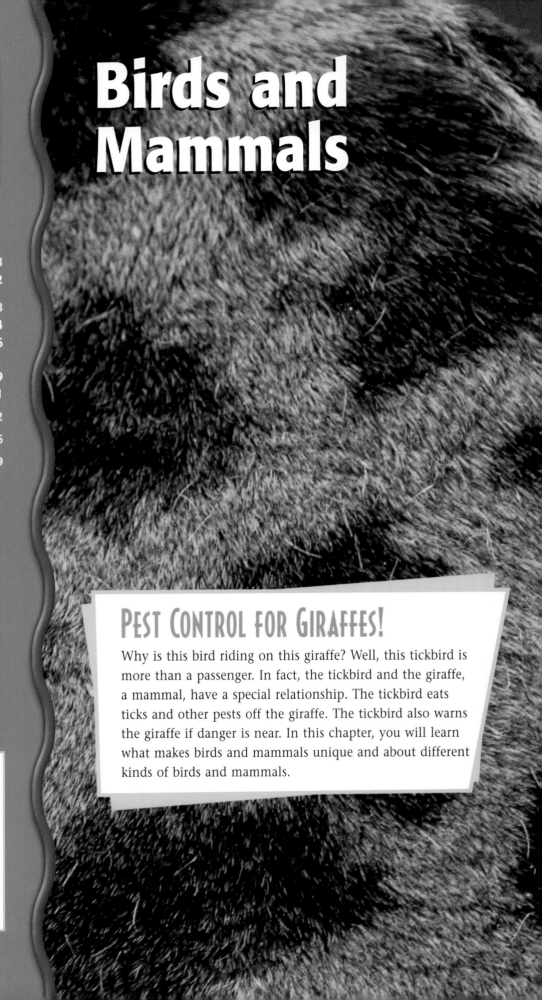

Birds and Mammals

Pre-Reading Questions

1. What holds a bird or plane up when it flies?

2. How do kangaroos differ from most other mammals?

3. Can mammals lay eggs? Can they fly?

Pest Control for Giraffes!

Why is this bird riding on this giraffe? Well, this tickbird is more than a passenger. In fact, the tickbird and the giraffe, a mammal, have a special relationship. The tickbird eats ticks and other pests off the giraffe. The tickbird also warns the giraffe if danger is near. In this chapter, you will learn what makes birds and mammals unique and about different kinds of birds and mammals.

LET'S FLY!

How do birds and airplanes fly? This activity will give you a few hints.

Procedure

1. Carefully fold a **piece of paper** to make a paper airplane. Make the folds even and the creases sharp.

2. Throw the plane very gently. What happened?

3. Take the same plane, and throw it more forcefully. Did anything change?

4. Reduce the size of the wings by folding them inward, toward the center crease. Make sure the two wings are the same size and shape.

5. Throw the airplane again, first gently and with more force. What happened each time?

Analysis

6. Analyze what effect the force of your throw has on the paper airplane's flight. Do you think this is true of bird flight? Explain.

7. What happened when the wings were made smaller? Why do you think this happened? Do you think wing size affects the way a bird flies?

8. Based on your results, how would you design and throw the perfect paper airplane? Explain your answer.

Terms to Learn

down feather   lift
contour feather   brooding
preening

What You'll Do

◆ Name two characteristics that birds share with reptiles.
◆ Describe the characteristics of birds that make them well suited for flight.
◆ Explain *lift.*
◆ List some advantages of migration.

Birds

Have you ever fed pigeons in a city park or watched a hawk fly in circles in the sky? Humans have always been birdwatchers, perhaps because birds are easier to recognize than almost any other animal. Unlike other animals, all birds have feathers. Birds are also well known for their ability to fly. Birds belong to the class Aves. The word *aves* comes from the Latin word for bird. In fact, the word *aviation*—the science of flying airplanes—comes from the same word.

Great blue heron

Figure 1 *There are almost 9,000 species of birds on Earth today.*

Toucan

Hummingbird

Bird Characteristics

The first birds appeared on Earth about 150 million years ago. Birds are thought to be descendants of dinosaurs.

Even today birds share some characteristics with reptiles. Like reptiles, birds are vertebrates. The legs and feet of birds are covered by thick, dry scales, like those of reptiles. Even the skin around their beaks is scaly. Like reptiles, birds have *amniotic eggs,* that is, eggs with an amniotic sac and a shell. However, the shells of bird eggs are generally harder than the leathery shells of turtles and lizards.

Birds also have many characteristics that set them apart from the rest of the animal kingdom. They have beaks instead of teeth and jaws, and they have feathers, wings, and many other adaptations for flight.

Birds of a Feather Birds have two main types of feathers—down feathers and contour feathers. Examples of each are shown in **Figure 2.** Because feathers wear out, birds shed their worn feathers and grow new ones.

Figure 2 *Birds have light, fluffy down feathers and leaf-shaped contour feathers.*

Down feathers are fluffy, insulating feathers that lie next to a bird's body. To keep from losing heat, birds fluff up their down feathers to form a layer of insulation. Air trapped in the feathers helps keep birds warm. **Contour feathers** are made of a stiff central *shaft* with many side branches, called *barbs.* The barbs link together to form a smooth surface, as can be seen in **Figure 3.** Contour feathers cover the body and wings of birds to form a streamlined flying surface.

Birds take good care of their feathers. They use their beaks to spread oil on their feathers in a process called **preening.** The oil is secreted by a gland near the bird's tail. The oil helps make the feathers water repellent and keeps them clean.

Shaft

Barbs

Barbules

Figure 3 *The barbs of a contour feather have cross branches called barbules. Barbs and barbules give the feather strength and shape.*

High-Energy Animals Birds need a lot of energy in order to fly. To get this energy, they have a high metabolism, which generates a lot of body heat. In fact, the average body temperature of a bird is 40°C, warmer than yours! If birds are too hot, they lay their feathers flat and pant like dogs do. Birds cannot sweat to cool their bodies.

Eat Like a Bird? Because of their high metabolism, birds eat large amounts of food in proportion to their body weight. Some small birds eat almost constantly to maintain their energy! Most birds eat a high-protein, high-fat diet of insects, nuts, seeds, or meat. This kind of diet requires only a small digestive tract. A few birds, such as geese, eat the leaves of plants.

Birds don't have teeth, so they can't chew their food. Instead, food goes directly from the mouth to the *crop,* where it is stored. Birds also have an organ called a *gizzard,* which often contains small stones. The stones in the gizzard grind up the food so that it can be easily digested by the intestine. A bird's digestive system is shown in **Figure 4.**

Figure 4 *The digestive system of a bird allows food to be rapidly converted into usable energy.*

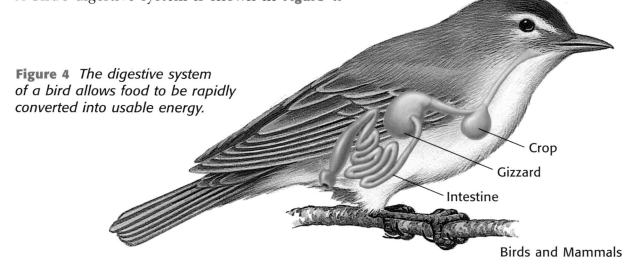

Crop

Gizzard

Intestine

Self-Check

1. Why don't birds have wings made of down feathers?
2. Why do birds eat large quantities of food?

(See page 152 to check your answers.)

Up, Up, and Away

Most birds are flyers. Even flightless birds, such as ostriches, are descended from ancestors that could fly.

Birds have a long list of adaptations for flight. Birds must take in a large amount of energy from the food they eat and a large amount of oxygen from the air they breathe in order to fly. Feathers and wings are also important, as are strong muscles. Birds have lightweight bodies so that they can get off the ground. **Figure 5** on these two pages explains many of the bird characteristics that are important for flight.

Figure 5 Flight Adaptations of Birds

Most birds have **large eyes** and excellent eyesight. This allows them to see objects and food from a distance. Some birds, like hawks and eagles, can see eight times better than humans!

Air sacs

Lung

The **heart** of a bird beats rapidly. This ensures that the flight muscles get as much oxygen as the blood can carry. In small birds, the heart beats almost 1,000 times a minute! Your heart beats about 70 times a minute.

Birds have special organs called **air sacs** attached to their lungs. The air sacs increase the amount of oxygen that a bird can take in and allow air to flow constantly in one direction through the lungs.

The shape of a bird's **wings** is related to the kind of flying it does. Short, rounded wings allow rapid maneuvers, like the movements of a fighter plane. Long narrow wings are best for soaring, like the movement of a glider.

Science CONNECTION

These characteristics help birds fly, but how do airplanes fly? Find out on page 118.

Bird skeletons are compact and strong. Some of the vertebrae, ribs, and hip bones are fused together. This makes the skeleton of birds more rigid than that of other vertebrates. The **rigid skeleton** lets a bird move its wings powerfully and efficiently.

Keel

Birds that fly have powerful **flight muscles** attached to a large breastbone called a **keel**. These muscles move the wings.

Bone is a heavy material, but birds have much **lighter skeletons** than those of other vertebrates because their bones are hollow. But bird bones are still very strong because they have thin cross-supports that provide strength, much like the trusses of a bridge do.

Bernoulli Effect

Is it true that fast-moving air creates low pressure? You bet. You can see this effect easily with a straw and a piece of paper. First find a partner. Use a **pin** to make a hole in one side of a **drinking straw.** Cut or tear a small strip of **paper** about 3 cm long and 0.5 cm wide. Hold the strip of paper as close to the hole as you can without letting the paper touch the straw. Ask your partner to blow into the straw. The fast-moving air will create low pressure in the straw. The higher air pressure in the room will push the paper against the hole. Try it!

Getting off the Ground

How do birds overcome gravity and fly? Birds flap their wings to get into the air and to push themselves through the air. Wings provide lift. **Lift** is the upward pressure on the wing that keeps a bird in the air.

When air flows past a wing, some of the air is forced over the top of the wing, and some is forced underneath. A bird's wing is curved on top. As shown in **Figure 6,** the air on top has to move *farther* than the air underneath. As a result, the air on top moves *faster* than the air underneath. The fast-moving air on top creates low pressure in the air. This is called the *Bernoulli effect.* The air pressure under the wing is higher and pushes the wing up.

Figure 6 *A bird's wing is shaped to produce lift. Air moving over the top of the wing moves faster than air moving underneath the wing. This creates a difference in air pressure that keeps a bird in the air.*

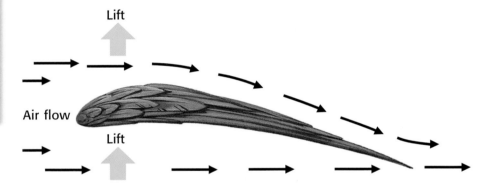

Birds generate extra lift by flapping their wings. The faster a bird flies, the greater the lift. Another factor that affects lift is wing size. The larger the wing, the greater the lift. This is why birds with large wings can soar long distances without flapping their wings. An albatross, like the one in **Figure 7,** can glide over the ocean for many hours without flapping its wings.

Figure 7 *The wandering albatross has a wingspan of 3.5 m, the largest of any living bird. Its large wings allow the albatross to glide for very long periods of time. An albatross comes ashore only to lay its eggs.*

Fly Away

It is sometimes said that when the going gets tough, the tough get going. If that's true, birds must be some of the toughest animals in the world. For when times are hard, some birds get going faster and farther than any other animal. Because they are able to fly great distances, birds are able to migrate great distances.

Some birds have good reasons to migrate. By migrating, they can find better territories with more food. For example, in the far north in the summer, the Arctic sun is up nearly 24 hours a day. Plants, insects, and other organisms increase explosively, providing lots of food. It's a great place for birds to raise their young. However, the winters are long and harsh, and there is little to eat. So when winter comes, birds fly south to find better feeding grounds.

Bringing Up Baby

Like reptiles, birds reproduce by internal fertilization and lay amniotic eggs with the developing embryo inside. But unlike most reptiles, birds must keep their eggs warm for the embryo to develop.

Most birds build elaborate nests and lay their eggs inside them. **Figure 8** shows a few of the many different kinds of bird nests. Birds sit on their eggs until the eggs hatch, using their body heat to keep the eggs warm. This is called **brooding.** Some birds, such as gulls, share brooding duties equally between males and females. But among songbirds, the female is in charge of brooding the eggs, and the male brings her food.

Raising young birds is hard work. Some birds, such as cuckoos and cowbirds, have found a way to make other birds do their work for them. A cuckoo lays its eggs in the nest of another species of bird. When the cuckoo egg hatches, the young cuckoo is fed and protected by the foster parents.

Figure 8 *There are many different types of bird nests. Birds use grass, branches, mud, hair, feathers, and many other building materials.*

Figure 9 *Precocial chicks learn to recognize their parents right after they hatch. But if their parents are not there, the chicks will follow the first moving thing they see, even a person.*

Ready to Go Some baby birds hatch from the egg ready to run around and eat bugs. Chicks that hatch fully active are *precocial* (pree KOH shuhl). Chickens, ducks, and shorebirds all hatch precocial chicks. Precocial chicks are covered with downy feathers and follow their parents as soon as they can stand up. You can see some precocial chicks following a stand-in parent in **Figure 9**. Precocial chicks depend on their mother for warmth and protection, but they can walk, swim, and feed themselves.

Help Wanted The chicks of hawks, songbirds, and many other birds hatch weak, naked, and helpless. These chicks are *altricial* (al TRISH uhl). Their eyes are closed when they are born. Newly hatched altricial chicks cannot walk or fly. Their parents must keep them warm and feed them for several weeks. **Figure 10** shows altricial chicks being fed by a parent.

When altricial chicks grow their first flight feathers, they begin learning to fly. This takes days, however, and the chicks often end up walking around on the ground. The parents must work feverishly to distract cats, weasels, and other predators and protect their young.

SECTION REVIEW

1. List three ways birds are similar to reptiles and three ways they are different.

2. Explain the difference between precocial chicks and altricial chicks.

3. People use the phrase "eats like a bird" to describe someone who eats very little. Is this saying appropriate? Why or why not?

4. Name some of the adaptations that make bird bodies lightweight.

5. **Understanding Technology** Would an airplane wing that is not curved on top generate lift? Draw a picture to illustrate your explanation.

Figure 10 *Both parents of altricial chicks leave the nest in search of food. They return to the nest with food every few minutes, sometimes making 1,000 trips a day between the two of them!*

Kinds of Birds

There are almost 9,000 species of birds on Earth. Birds range in size from the 1.6 g bee hummingbird to the 125 kg North African ostrich. The bodies of birds have different characteristics too, depending on where they live and what they eat. Because of their great diversity, birds are classified into 29 different orders. That can be confusing, so birds are often grouped into four nonscientific categories: flightless birds, water birds, birds of prey, and perching birds. These categories don't include all birds, but they do show how different birds can be.

BRAIN FOOD

An ostrich egg has a mass of about 1.4 kg. A single ostrich egg is big enough to provide scrambled eggs for a family of four every morning for several days.

Flightless Birds

Ostriches, kiwis, emus, and other flightless birds do not have a large keel for flight. Though they cannot fly, many flightless birds are fast runners.

▲ The **kiwi,** of New Zealand, is a forest bird about the size of a chicken. Its feathers are soft and hair-like. Kiwis sleep during the day. At night, they hunt for worms, caterpillars, and berries.

▲ **Penguins** are unique flightless birds. They have a large keel and very strong flight muscles, but their wings have been modified into flippers. They flap these wings to swim underwater. Although penguins are graceful swimmers, they walk clumsily on land.

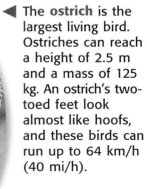

◀ The **ostrich** is the largest living bird. Ostriches can reach a height of 2.5 m and a mass of 125 kg. An ostrich's two-toed feet look almost like hoofs, and these birds can run up to 64 km/h (40 mi/h).

Water Birds

Water birds are sometimes called *waterfowl.* These include cranes, ducks, geese, swans, pelicans, loons, and many other species. These birds usually have webbed feet for swimming, but they are also strong flyers.

Male **wood ducks** have beautiful ▶ plumage to attract females. Like all ducks, they are strong swimmers and flyers.

◀ The **blue-footed booby** is a tropical water bird. These birds have an elaborate courtship dance that includes raising their feet one at a time.

The **common loon** is the ▶ most primitive of modern birds. It can remain underwater for several minutes while searching for fish.

Birds of Prey

Eagles, hawks, falcons, and other birds of prey are meat eaters. They may eat mammals, fish, reptiles, birds, or other animals. The sharp claws on their feet and their sharp, curved beaks help these birds catch and eat their prey. They also have very good vision. Most birds of prey hunt during the day.

◀ Owls, like this **northern spotted owl,** are the only birds of prey that hunt at night. They have a keen sense of hearing to help them find their prey.

▲ **Ospreys** are fish eaters. They fly over the water and catch fish with their feet.

Perching Birds

Songbirds, like robins, wrens, warblers, and sparrows, are perching birds. These birds have special adaptations for perching on a branch. When a perching bird lands on a branch, its feet automatically close around the branch. So even if the bird falls asleep, it will not fall off.

▲ **Parrots** are not songbirds, but they have special feet for perching and climbing. Their strong, hooked beak allows them to open seeds and slice fruit.

▲ **Chickadees** are lively little birds that frequently flock to garden feeders. They often dangle underneath a branch while hunting for insects, seeds, or fruits.

Most tanagers are tropical birds, ▶ but the **scarlet tanager** spends the summer in North America. The male is red, but the female is a yellow-green color that blends into the trees.

SECTION REVIEW

1. How did perching birds get their name?

2. Birds of prey have extremely good eyesight. Why is good vision important for these birds?

3. **Interpreting Illustrations** Look at the illustrations of bird feet at right. Which foot belongs to a water bird? a perching bird? Explain your answers.

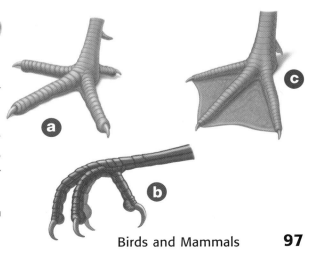

Terms to Learn

mammary glands   placental
diaphragm   mammal
monotreme   gestation period
marsupial

What You'll Do

◆ Describe common characteristics of mammals.
◆ Explain the differences between monotremes, marsupials, and placental mammals.
◆ Give some examples of each type of mammal.

Mammals

Of all the vertebrates, we seem most interested in mammals. Maybe that's because we are mammals ourselves. But with about 4,500 species, mammals are actually a small class of animals. Mollusks, for example, include more than 90,000 species.

Mammals come in many different forms—from the tiniest bats, which weigh less than a cracker, to the largest whales. The blue whale, with a mass of more than 90,000 kg, is the largest animal—vertebrate or invertebrate—that has ever lived. You can find mammals in the coldest oceans, in the hottest deserts, and in every climate in between. You can see some of the variety of mammals in **Figure 11.**

Rhinoceros

Figure 11 *Even though they look very different, all of these animals are mammals.*

Beluga whale

Mandrill baboon

The Origin of Mammals

Fossil evidence suggests that about 280 million years ago, mammal-like reptiles called therapsids appeared. *Therapsids* (thuh RAP sidz) were the early ancestors of mammals. An artist's rendition of a therapsid is shown in **Figure 12.**

About 200 million years ago, the first mammals appeared in the fossil record. These mammals were about the size of mice. The early mammals were endotherms. Because they did not depend on their surroundings for heat, they could forage at night and avoid their dinosaur predators during the day.

When the dinosaurs became extinct, there was more land and food available for the mammals. Mammals began to diversify and live in many different environments.

Figure 12 *Therapsids had characteristics of both reptiles and mammals and may have looked something like this.*

Characteristics of Mammals

Dolphins and elephants are mammals, and so are monkeys, horses, and rabbits. You are a mammal, too! These animals are very different, but all mammals share many distinctive traits.

Mamma! All mammals have mammary glands; this sets them apart from other animals. **Mammary glands** secrete a nutritious fluid called milk. All female mammals supply milk to their young. Female mammals usually bear live young and care for their offspring, as illustrated in **Figure 13.** Although only mature female mammals make milk, male mammals also have small inactive mammary glands.

Figure 13 *Like all mammals, this calf gets its first meals from its mother's milk.*

All milk is made of water, protein, fat, and sugar. But the milk from different mammals has varying amounts of each nutrient. For example, human milk has half as much fat as cow's milk but twice as much sugar. The milk of seals may be more than one-half fat. At birth, elephant seals have a mass of 45 kg. After drinking this rich milk for just 3 weeks, their mass is 180 kg!

Cozy and Warm If you've ever had a dog fall asleep in your lap, you already know that mammals are really warm! All mammals are endotherms. Like birds, mammals require a lot of energy from the food they eat. Mammals quickly break down food in their bodies and use the energy released from their cells to keep their bodies warm. Usually a mammal keeps its body temperature constant. Only when a mammal is hibernating, estivating, or running a fever does its body temperature change.

Figure 14 *Mammals feel warm to the touch because they are endotherms.*

Figure 15 *The thick fur of this arctic fox keeps its body warm in even the coldest winters.*

Figure 16
Mountain lions have sharp canine teeth for grabbing their prey. Donkeys have sharp incisors in front for cutting plants and flat grinding teeth in the back of their mouth.

Staying Warm Mammals have adaptations to help them keep warm. One way they stay warm is by having a thick coat, and many mammals have luxurious coats of fur. All mammals, even whales, have hair somewhere on their body. This is another trait that sets mammals apart from other animals. Mammals that live in cold climates usually have thick coats of hair, such as the fox in **Figure 15.** But large mammals that live in warm climates, like elephants, have less hair. Gorillas and humans have similar amounts of hair on their bodies, but human hair is finer and shorter.

Most mammals also have a layer of fat under the skin that acts as insulation. Whales and other mammals that live in cold oceans depend on a layer of fat called *blubber* to keep them warm.

Crunch! Another trait that sets mammals apart from other animals is their teeth. Birds don't even have teeth! And although fish and reptiles have teeth, their teeth tend to be all alike. In contrast, most mammals' teeth are specialized. They have different shapes and sizes for different functions.

Let's look at your teeth, for example. The teeth in the front of your mouth are cutting teeth, called *incisors.* Most people have four on top and four on the bottom. The next teeth are stabbing teeth, called *canines.* Canines help you grab food and hold onto it. Farther back in your mouth are flat teeth called *molars* that help grind up food.

The kinds of teeth a mammal has reflect its diet. Dogs, cats, wolves, foxes, and other meat-eating mammals have large canines. Molars are better developed in animals that eat plants. **Figure 16** shows the teeth of different mammals.

Unlike other vertebrates, mammals have two sets of teeth. A young mammal's first small teeth are called *milk teeth.* These are replaced by a set of permanent adult teeth after the mammal begins eating solid food and its jaw grows larger.

Getting Oxygen Just as a fire needs oxygen in order to burn, all animals need oxygen to efficiently "burn," or break down, the food they eat. Like birds and reptiles, mammals use lungs to get oxygen from the air. But mammals also have a large muscle to help bring air into their lungs. This muscle is called the **diaphragm,** and it lies at the bottom of the rib cage.

Large Brains The brain of a mammal is much larger than the brain of another animal the same size. This allows mammals to learn, move, and think quickly. A mammal's highly developed brain also helps it keep track of what is going on in its environment and respond quickly.

Mammals depend on five major senses to provide them with information about their environment: vision, hearing, smell, touch, and taste. The importance of each sense for any given mammal often depends on the mammal's environment. For example, mammals that are active at night rely more heavily on their ability to hear than on their ability to see.

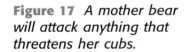

Activity

Like all mammals, you have a diaphragm. Place your hand underneath your rib cage. What happens as you breathe in and out? You are feeling the motion of your abdominal muscles, which are connected to your diaphragm. Contract and relax your abdominal muscles. What happens?

TRY at HOME

Mammal Parents All mammals reproduce sexually. Like birds and reptiles, mammals reproduce by internal fertilization. Most mammals give birth to live young, and all mammals nurse their young. Mammal parents are very protective, with one or both parents caring for their young until they are grown. **Figure 17** shows a brown bear caring for its young.

Figure 17 A mother bear will attack anything that threatens her cubs.

SECTION REVIEW

1. Name three characteristics that are unique to mammals.

2. What is the purpose of a diaphragm?

3. **Making Inferences** Suppose you found a mammal skull on an archaeological dig. How would the teeth give you clues about the mammal's diet?

Kinds of Mammals

Mammals are divided into three groups based on the way their young develop. These groups are monotremes, marsupials, and placental mammals.

Figure 18 *Echidnas are about the size of a house cat. They have large claws and long snouts that help them dig ants and termites out of their nests.*

Monotremes Mammals that lay eggs are called **monotremes.** Monotremes are the only mammals that lay eggs, and early scientists called them "furred reptiles." But monotremes are not reptiles; they have all the mammal traits. They have mammary glands and a thick fur coat, and they are endotherms.

A female monotreme lays eggs with thick, leathery shells. Like bird and reptile eggs, monotreme eggs have a yolk and albumen to feed the developing embryo. The female incubates the eggs with her body heat. Newly hatched young are not fully developed. The mother protects her young and feeds them milk. Unlike other mammals, monotremes do not have nipples, and the babies cannot suck. Instead, the tiny monotremes nurse by licking milk from the skin and hair around their mother's mammary glands.

Two Kinds of Monotremes Monotremes are found only in Australia and New Guinea, and just three species of monotremes are alive today. Two are echidnas (ee KID nuhs), spine-covered animals with long snouts. Echidnas have long sticky tongues for catching ants and termites. You can see an echidna in **Figure 18.**

The third monotreme is the duckbilled platypus, shown in **Figure 19.** The duckbilled platypus is a swimming mammal that lives and feeds in rivers and ponds. It has webbed feet and a flat tail to help it move through the water. It also has a flat, rubbery bill that it uses to dig for food and to dig long tunnels in riverbanks to lay its eggs.

Figure 19 *When underwater, a duckbilled platypus closes its eyes and ears. It uses its sensitive bill to find food.*

Marsupials You probably know that kangaroos, like those in **Figure 20,** have pouches. Kangaroos are **marsupials,** mammals with pouches. Like all mammals, marsupials are endotherms. They have mammary glands, fur, and teeth. Unlike the monotremes, marsupials do not lay eggs. They give birth to live young.

Like newly hatched monotremes, marsupial infants are not fully developed. At birth, the tiny embryos of a kangaroo are no larger than bumblebees. Shortly after birth, they drag themselves through their mother's fur until they reach a pouch on her abdomen. Inside the pouch are mammary glands. The young kangaroo climbs in, latches onto a nipple, and drinks milk until it is able to move around by itself and leave the pouch for short periods. Young kangaroos are called joeys.

There are about 280 species of marsupials. The only marsupial in North America north of Mexico is the opossum (uh PAHS suhm), shown in **Figure 21.** Other marsupials include koalas, shown in **Figure 22,** Tasmanian devils, and wallabies. Most marsupials live in Australia, New Guinea, and South America.

Figure 20 *After birth, a kangaroo continues to develop in its mother's pouch. Older joeys leave the pouch but return if there is any sign of danger.*

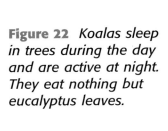

Figure 21 *When in danger, an opossum will lie perfectly still and pretend to be dead so predators will tend to ignore it.*

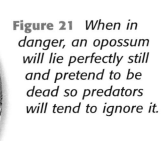

Figure 22 *Koalas sleep in trees during the day and are active at night. They eat nothing but eucalyptus leaves.*

BRAIN FOOD

When a kangaroo first climbs into its mother's pouch, the mother's milk is nonfat. Later, the milk is about 20 percent fat. A mother kangaroo with two babies that are different ages supplies nonfat milk to the baby and fat milk to the older one. Each youngster nurses from a different nipple.

Placental Mammals Most mammals are placental mammals. In **placental mammals,** the embryos stay inside the mother's body and develop in an organ called the *uterus.* Placental embryos form a special attachment to the uterus of their mother called a *placenta.* The placenta supplies food and oxygen from the mother's blood to the growing embryo. The placenta also removes wastes from the embryo.

The time during which an embryo develops within the mother is called the **gestation period.** Gestation (jeh STAY shuhn) periods in placental animals range from a few weeks in mice to as long as 23 months in elephants. Humans have a gestation period of about 9 months.

✓ Self-Check

Explain the difference between a monotreme, a marsupial, and a placental mammal. *(See page 152 to check your answer.)*

Kinds of Placental Mammals

Over 90 percent of all the mammals on Earth are placental mammals. Living placental mammals are classified into 18 orders. The characteristics of the most common orders are given on the following pages.

Toothless Mammals

This group includes anteaters, armadillos, aardvarks, pangolins, and sloths. Although these mammals are called "toothless," only the anteaters are completely tooth-less. The others have small teeth. Most toothless mammals feed on insects they catch with their long sticky tongues.

Armadillos eat ▶ insects, frogs, mush-rooms, and roots. When threatened, an armadillo rolls up into a ball and is protected by its tough plates.

▲ The largest anteater is the 40 kg **giant anteater** of South America. Anteaters never destroy the nests of their prey. They open the nests, eat a few ants or termites, and then move on to another nest.

Insect Eaters

Insect eaters, or *insectivores,* live on every continent except Australia and Antarctica. Most insectivores are small, and most have long pointed noses to dig into the soil for food. Compared with other mammals, they have a very small brain and few specialized teeth. Insectivores include moles, shrews, and hedgehogs.

◄ The **star-nosed mole** has sensitive feelers on its nose to help it find insects and feel its way while burrowing underground. Although they have tiny eyes, moles cannot see.

▲ **Hedgehogs** live throughout Europe, Asia, and Africa. Their spines keep them safe from most predators.

Rodents

More than one-third of all mammalian species are rodents, and they can be found on every continent except Antarctica. Rodents include squirrels, mice, rats, guinea pigs, porcupines, and chinchillas. Most rodents are small animals with long, sensitive whiskers. Rodents are chewers and gnawers. All rodents have sharp front teeth for gnawing. Because rodents chew so much, their teeth wear down. So a rodent's incisors grow continuously, just like your fingernails do.

▲ The **capybaras** (KAP i BAH ruhs) of South America are the largest rodents in the world. A female can have a mass of 70 kg—as much as a grown man.

▲ Like all rodents, **beavers** have gnawing teeth. They use these teeth to cut down trees.

Lagomorphs

Rabbits, hares, and pikas belong to a group of placental mammals called lagomorphs. Like rodents, they have sharp gnawing teeth. But unlike rodents, they have two sets of incisors in their upper jaw and short tails. Rabbits and hares have long, powerful hind legs for jumping. To detect their many predators, they have sensitive noses and large ears and eyes.

◀ **Pikas** are small animals that live high in the mountains. Pikas gather plants and mound them in "haystacks" to dry. In the winter, they use the dry plants for food and insulation.

▲ The large ears of this **black-tailed jack rabbit** help it hear well.

Flying Mammals

Bats are the only mammals that can fly. Bats are active at night and sleep in sheltered areas during the day. Most bats eat insects. But some bats eat fruit, and three species of vampire bats drink the blood of other animals.

Most bats hunt for insects at night. They find their way using echolocation. Bats make clicking noises when they fly. Trees, rocks, insects, and other objects reflect the sound back to the bat, making an echo.

Echoes from a big, hard tree sound very different from those reflecting off a soft, tasty moth. Bats that echolocate often have enormous ears to help them hear the echoes of their own clicks.

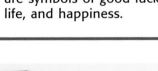

In many Asian countries, **bats** ▶ are symbols of good luck, long life, and happiness.

Bats and Submarines

What do bats have in common with submarines? Submarines use a form of echolocation called sonar to find and avoid objects underwater. Based on what you know about echolocation, what kind of instruments do you think are needed to navigate a submarine with sonar?

Carnivores

Carnivores are a group of mammals that have large canines and special teeth for slicing meat. The name *carnivore* means "meat eater"—the mammals in this group primarily eat meat. Carnivorous mammals include lions, wolves, weasels, otters, bears, raccoons, and hyenas. Carnivores also include a group of fish-eating marine mammals called *pinnipeds.* The pinnipeds include seals, sea lions, and walruses. Some carnivores also eat plants. For example, black bears eat grass, nuts, and berries and only rarely eat meat. But many carnivores eat nothing but other animals.

▲ **Coyotes** are members of the dog family. They live throughout North America and in parts of Central America.

▼ **Raccoons** have handlike paws that help them catch fish and hold their food. They can handle objects almost as well as monkeys can.

▲ Cats are divided into two groups, big cats and small cats. All the big cats can roar. The largest of the big cats is the **Siberian tiger,** with a mass of up to 300 kg.

◄ **Walruses** are pinnipeds. Unlike other carnivores, walruses do not use their canines for tearing food. Instead, they use them to defend themselves, to dig for food, and to climb on ice.

Hoofed Mammals

Horses, pigs, deer, and rhinoceroses are just a few of the many mammals that have thick hoofs. Most hoofed mammals are adapted for swift running. Because they are plant eaters, they have large, flat molars to help them grind plant material.

Hoofed mammals are divided into groups based on the number of toes they have. Odd-toed hoofed mammals have one or three toes. Horses and zebras have a single large hoof, or toe. Other odd-toed hoofed mammals include rhinoceroses and tapirs. Even-toed hoofed mammals have two or four toes. These mammals include pigs, cows, camels, deer, hippopotamuses, and giraffes.

▲ **Giraffes** are the tallest living mammals. They have long necks, long legs, and an even number of toes.

▲ **Tapirs** are large, three-toed mammals that live in forests. Tapirs can be found in Central America, South America, and Southeast Asia.

Camels are even- ▶ toed mammals. The hump of a camel is a large lump of fat that provides energy for the camel when food is scarce.

Trunk-Nosed Mammals

Elephants are the only mammals with a trunk. The trunk is an elongated and muscular combination of the upper lip and nose. Elephants use their trunk the same way we use our hands, lips, and nose. The trunk is powerful enough to lift a tree yet agile enough to pick small fruits one at a time. Elephants use their trunk to place food in their mouth and to spray their back with water to cool off.

There are two species of elephants, African elephants and Asian elephants. African elephants are larger and have bigger ears and tusks than Asian elephants. Both species eat plants. Because they are so large, elephants eat up to 18 hours a day to get enough food.

Elephants are the largest land animals. Male African elephants can reach a mass of 7,500 kg! Elephants are very intelligent and may live more than 60 years.

▼ **Elephants** are social animals. They live in herds of related females and their offspring. The whole family helps take care of young.

Environment CONNECTION

Both species of elephants are endangered. For centuries, humans have hunted elephants for their long teeth, called tusks. Elephant tusks are made of ivory, a hard material used for carving. Because of the high demand for ivory, much of the elephant population has been wiped out. Today elephant hunting is illegal.

Cetaceans

Whales, dolphins, and porpoises make up a group of water-dwelling mammals called cetaceans (see TAY shuhns). At first glance, whales and their relatives may look more like fish than mammals. But like all mammals, cetaceans are endotherms, have lungs, and nurse their young. Most of the largest whales are toothless whales that strain tiny, shrimp-like animals from sea water. But dolphins, porpoises, sperm whales, and killer whales have teeth, which they use to eat fish and other animals.

▲ **Spinner dolphins** spin like a football when they leap from the water. Like all dolphins, they are intelligent and highly social.

◄ Like bats, cetaceans use echolocation to "see" their surroundings. **Sperm whales**, like this one, use loud blasts of sound to stun fish, making them easier to catch.

Sirenia

The smallest group of water-dwelling mammals is called sirenia (sie REE nee uh). It includes just four species—three kinds of manatees and the dugong. These mammals are completely aquatic; they live along coasts and in large rivers. They are quiet animals that eat seaweed and water plants.

Manatees are also ► called sea cows.

Primates

Prosimians, monkeys, apes, and humans all belong to a group of mammals called *primates.* There are about 160 species of primates. All primates have the eyes facing forward, enabling both eyes to focus on a single point. Most primates have five fingers on each hand and five toes on each foot, with flat fingernails instead of claws. Primates' fingers and opposable thumbs are able to make complicated movements, like grasping objects. Primates have a large brain in proportion to their body size and are considered some of the most intelligent mammals.

Many primates live in trees. Their flexible shoulder joints and grasping hands and feet enable them to climb trees and swing from branch to branch. Most primates eat a diet of leaves and fruits, but some also eat animals.

◀ **Spider monkeys,** like most monkeys, have grasping tails. Their long arms, legs, and tails help them move among the trees.

▲ **Orangutans** and other apes frequently walk upright. Apes usually have larger brains and bodies than monkeys.

SECTION REVIEW

1. If you saw only the feet of a hippopotamus and a rhinoceros, could you tell the difference between the two animals? Explain your answer.

2. How are monotremes different from all other mammals? How are they similar?

3. To what group of placental mammals do dogs belong? How do you know?

4. **Making Inferences** What is a gestation period? Why do elephants have a longer gestation period than do mice?

internetconnect

SCiLINKS.
NSTA

TOPIC: The Origin of Mammals, Characteristics of Mammals
GO TO: www.scilinks.org
*sci*LINKS NUMBER: HSTL415, HSTL420

Making Models Lab

What? No Dentist Bills?

When you eat, you must chew your food well. Chewing food into small bits is the first part of digestion. But birds don't have teeth. How do birds make big chunks of food small enough to begin digestion? In this activity, you will develop a hypothesis about how birds digest their food. Then you will build a model of a bird's digestive system to test your hypothesis.

Ask a Question

1 How are birds able to begin digestion without having any teeth?

Form a Hypothesis

2 Look at the diagram below of a bird's digestive system. Form a hypothesis that answers the question above. Write your hypothesis in your ScienceLog.

MATERIALS

- several resealable plastic bags of various sizes
- birdseed
- aquarium gravel
- water
- string
- drinking straw
- transparent tape
- scissors or other materials as needed

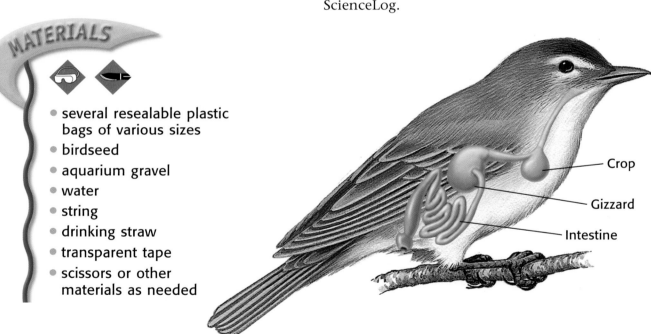

Crop

Gizzard

Intestine

Test the Hypothesis

3 Design a model of a bird's digestive system using the materials listed on page 112. Include in your design as many of these parts as possible: esophagus, crop, gizzard, intestine, and cloaca.

4 Using the materials you selected, build your model.

5 Test your model with the birdseed. Record your observations.

Analyze the Results

6 Did your "gizzard" grind the food?

7 What do you think *gizzard stones* are? How do you think they help a bird?

8 Does the amount of material added to your model gizzard change its ability to work effectively? Explain your answer.

9 Birds can break down food particles without teeth. What conclusions can you draw about how they do this?

Draw Conclusions

10 Analyze the strengths and weaknesses of your hypothesis based on your results. Was your hypothesis correct? Explain your answer.

11 What are some limitations of your model? How do you think you could improve it?

Going Further
Did you know that scientists have found "gizzard stones" with fossilized dinosaur skeletons? Look in the library or on the Internet for information about the evolutionary relationship between dinosaurs and birds. List the similarities and differences you find between these two types of animals.

Chapter Highlights

Vocabulary

down feather *(p. 89)*

contour feather *(p. 89)*

preening *(p. 89)*

lift *(p. 92)*

brooding *(p. 93)*

Section Notes

- Like reptiles, birds lay amniotic eggs and have thick, dry scales.

- Unlike reptiles, birds are endotherms and are covered with feathers.

- Because flying requires a lot of energy, birds must eat a high-energy diet and breathe efficiently.

- Birds' wings are shaped so that they generate lift. Lift is air pressure beneath the wings that keeps a bird in the air.

- Birds are lightweight. Their feathers are strong but lightweight, and their skeleton is relatively rigid, compact, and hollow.

- Because birds can fly, they can migrate great distances. They can nest in one habitat and winter in another. Migrating birds can take advantage of food supplies and avoid predators.

☑ Skills Check

Visual Understanding

LIFT The diagram on page 92 helps explain the concept of lift. Looking at this illustration, you can see that air must travel a greater distance over a curved wing than under a curved wing. The air above the wing must move faster than the air underneath in order to cover the greater distance in the same amount of time. Faster-moving air creates lower pressure above the wing. The higher pressure under the wing forces it up, creating lift.

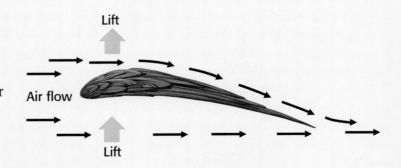

Vocabulary

mammary glands *(p. 99)*

diaphragm *(p. 101)*

monotreme *(p. 102)*

marsupial *(p. 103)*

placental mammal *(p. 104)*

gestation period *(p. 104)*

Section Notes

- All mammals have mammary glands; in females, mammary glands produce milk. Milk is a highly nutritious fluid fed to the young.

- Like birds, mammals are endotherms.

- Mammals maintain their high metabolism by eating a lot of food and breathing efficiently.

- Mammals have a diaphragm that helps them draw air into their lungs.

- Mammals have highly specialized teeth for chewing different kinds of food. Mammals that eat plants have incisors and molars for cutting and grinding plants. Carnivores have canines for seizing and tearing their prey.

- Mammals are the only vertebrates that have mammary glands, fur, and two sets of teeth.

- Mammals are divided into three groups: monotremes, marsupials, and placental mammals.

- Monotremes lay eggs instead of bearing live young. Monotremes produce milk but do not have nipples or a placenta.

- Marsupials give birth to live young, but the young are born as embryos. The embryos climb into their mother's pouch, where they drink milk until they are more developed.

- Placental mammals develop inside of the mother for a period of time called a gestation period. Placental mothers nurse their young after birth.

 internet**connect**

GO TO: go.hrw.com

Visit the **HRW** Web site for a variety of learning tools related to this chapter. Just type in the keyword:

KEYWORD: HSTVR2

 SCI*LINKS*ₛₘ

N S T A   **GO TO:** www.scilinks.org

Visit the **National Science Teachers Association** on-line Web site for Internet resources related to this chapter. Just type in the sci**LINKS** number for more information about the topic:

TOPIC: Bird Characteristics	*sci***LINKS NUMBER:** HSTL405
TOPIC: Kinds of Birds	*sci***LINKS NUMBER:** HSTL410
TOPIC: The Origin of Mammals	*sci***LINKS NUMBER:** HSTL415
TOPIC: Characteristics of Mammals	*sci***LINKS NUMBER:** HSTL420

Chapter Review

To complete the following sentences, choose the correct term from each pair of terms listed below:

1. __?__ chicks can run after their mother soon after they hatch. __?__ chicks can barely stretch their neck out to be fed when they first hatch. (*Altricial* or *Precocial*)

2. The __?__ helps mammals breathe. (*diaphragm* or *air sac*)

3. The __?__ allows some mammals to supply nutrients to young in the mother's uterus. (*mammary gland* or *placenta*)

4. Birds take care of their feathers by __?__. (*brooding* or *preening*)

5. A lion belongs to a group of mammals called __?__. (*carnivores* or *primates*)

6. __?__ are fluffy feathers that help keep birds warm. (*Contour feathers* or *Down feathers*)

UNDERSTANDING CONCEPTS

Multiple Choice

7. Both birds and reptiles
    a. lay eggs.
    b. brood their young.
    c. have air sacs.
    d. have feathers.

8. Flight requires
    a. a lot of energy and oxygen.
    b. a lightweight body.
    c. strong flight muscles.
    d. All of the above

9. Only mammals
    a. have glands.
    b. nurse their young.
    c. lay eggs.
    d. have teeth.

10. Monotremes do not
    a. have mammary glands.
    b. care for their young.
    c. have pouches.
    d. have fur.

11. Lift
    a. is air that travels over the top of a wing.
    b. is provided by air sacs.
    c. is the upward force on a wing that keeps a bird in the air.
    d. is created by pressure from the diaphragm.

12. Which of the following is not a primate?
    a. a lemur   c. a pika
    b. a human   d. a chimpanzee

Short Answer

13. How are marsupials different from other mammals? How are they similar?

14. Both birds and mammals are endotherms. How do they stay warm?

15. What is the Bernoulli effect?

16. Why do some bats have large ears?

Concept Mapping

17. Use the following terms to create a concept map: monotremes, endotherms, birds, mammals, mammary glands, placental mammals, marsupials, feathers, hair.

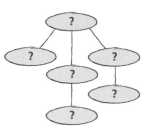

CRITICAL THINKING AND PROBLEM SOLVING

Write one or two sentences to answer the following questions:

18. Unlike bird and monotreme eggs, the eggs of placental mammals and marsupials do not have a yolk. How do developing embryos of marsupials and placental mammals get the nutrition they need?

19. Most bats and cetaceans use echolocation. Why don't these mammals rely solely on sight to find their prey and examine their surroundings?

20. Suppose you are working at a museum and are making a display of bird skeletons. Unfortunately, the skeletons have lost their labels. How can you separate the skeletons of flightless birds from those of birds that fly? Will you be able to tell which birds flew rapidly and which birds could soar? Explain your answer.

MATH IN SCIENCE

21. A bird is flying at a speed of 35 km/h. At this speed, its body consumes 60 Calories per gram of body mass per hour. If the bird has a mass of 50 g, how many Calories will it use if it flies for 30 minutes at this speed?

INTERPRETING GRAPHICS

Endotherms use a lot of energy when they run or fly. The graph below shows how many Calories a small dog uses while running at different speeds. Use this graph to answer the questions below.

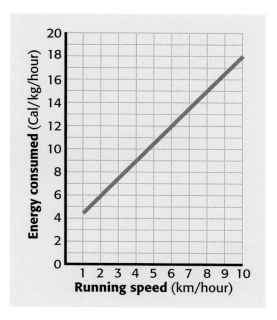

22. As the dog runs faster, how does the amount of energy it consumes per hour change?

23. How much energy per hour will this dog consume if it is running at 4 km/h? at 9 km/h?

24. Energy consumed is given in Calories per kilogram of body mass per hour. If the dog has a mass of 6 kg and is running at 7 km/h, how many Calories per hour will it use?

Reading Check-up

Take a minute to review your answers to the Pre-Reading Questions found at the bottom of page 86. Have your answers changed? If necessary, revise your answers based on what you have learned since you began this chapter.

The Aerodynamics of Flight

For centuries people have tried to imitate a spectacular feat that birds perfected millions of years ago—flight! It was not until 1903 that the Wright brothers were able to fly in a heavier-than-air flying machine. Their first flight lasted only 12 seconds, and they only traveled 37 m. Although modern airplanes are much more sophisticated, they still rely on the same principles of flight.

Fighting Gravity

The sleek body of a jet is shaped to battle drag, while the wings are shaped to battle Earth's gravity. In order to take off, airplanes must pull upward with a force greater than gravitational force. This upward force is called *lift.* Where does an airplane get lift? The top of an airplane wing is curved, and the bottom is flat. As the wing moves through the air, air must travel farther and faster above the wing than below it. This difference causes the pressure above the wing to be less than the pressure below the wing. This difference pulls the airplane upward.

Push and Pull

The shape of its wing is not enough to get an airplane off the ground. Wings require air to flow past them in order to create lift. Airplanes also rely on *thrust,* the force that gives an airplane forward motion. Powerful engines and propellers provide airplanes with thrust. As airplanes move faster, more air rushes past the wings, and lift increases.

Airplanes usually take off into a head wind, which pushes against the airplane as it travels. Any force that pushes against an airplane's motion, like a head wind, is called *drag* and can slow an airplane down. The body of an airplane has smooth curves to minimize drag. A tail wind is an airflow that pushes the airplane from the rear and shortens travel time. In order to increase speed, engineers design airplanes with streamlined bodies to reduce drag. Wings can also be designed to increase lift. A rounded and longer wing provides greater lift, but it also produces more drag. Engineers must consider such trade-offs when they design airplanes. Athletes also consider drag when they choose equipment. For example, runners and cyclists wear tight-fitting clothing to reduce drag.

Think About It!

▶ Airplanes have a variety of shapes and sizes and are designed for many purposes, including transport, travel, and combat. Some planes are designed to fly fast, and others are designed to carry heavy loads. Do some research, and then describe how the aerodynamics differ.

▲ *The design of airplanes got a boost from our feathered friends.*

NAKED MOLE-RATS

What do you call a nearly blind rodent that is 7 cm long and looks like a hot dog that has been left in the microwave too long? A naked mole-rat. For more than 150 years, this mammal—which is native to hot, dry regions of Kenya, Ethiopia, and Somalia—has puzzled scientists by its strange appearance and peculiar habits.

What's Hair Got to Do with It?

Naked mole-rats have such strange characteristics that you might wonder whether they are really mammals at all. Their grayish pink skin hangs loosely, allowing them to maneuver through the narrow underground tunnel systems they call home. At first glance, the naked mole-rats appear to be hairless, and hair is a key characteristic of mammals. However, naked mole-rats are not hairless, but they do lack fur. In fact, they have whiskers to guide them through the dark passages and hair between their toes to sweep up loose dirt like tiny brooms. Believe it or not, they also have hair on their lips to prevent dirt from entering their mouth as their massive teeth dig new passages through the dirt!

Is It Cold in Here?

Naked mole-rats have the poorest endothermic capacity of any mammal. Their body temperature remains close to the temperature of the air in their tunnels—a cool 31°C (more than 5°C cooler than the body temperature of humans). At night these animals minimize heat loss by huddling close together. Fortunately, the temperature does not change very much in their native habitat.

Who's in Charge?

Naked mole-rats are the only mammals known to form communities similar to those formed by social insects, such as honey bees. A community of naked mole-rats is made up of between 20 and 300 individuals that divide up tasks much like bees, wasps, and termites do. Each community has one breeding female, called the queen, and up to three breeding males. All females are biologically capable of reproducing, but only one does. When a female becomes a queen, she actually grows longer!

Think About It!

▶ At first glance, naked mole-rats appear to be missing several key characteristics of mammals. Do further research to find out what characteristics they have that classifies them as mammals.

◀ *Naked mole-rats are so unique that they have become a popular attraction at zoos.*

SAFETY FIRST!

Exploring, inventing, and investigating are essential to the study of science. However, these activities can also be dangerous. To make sure that your experiments and explorations are safe, you must be aware of a variety of safety guidelines.

You have probably heard of the saying, "It is better to be safe than sorry." This is particularly true in a science classroom where experiments and explorations are being performed. Being uninformed and careless can result in serious injuries. Don't take chances with your own safety or with anyone else's.

Following are important guidelines for staying safe in the science classroom. Your teacher may also have safety guidelines and tips that are specific to your classroom and laboratory. Take the time to be safe.

Safety Rules!

Start Out Right

Always get your teacher's permission before attempting any laboratory exploration. Read the procedures carefully, and pay particular attention to safety information and caution statements. If you are unsure about what a safety symbol means, look it up or ask your teacher. You cannot be too careful when it comes to safety. If an accident does occur, inform your teacher immediately, regardless of how minor you think the accident is.

Safety Symbols

All of the experiments and investigations in this book and their related worksheets include important safety symbols to alert you to particular safety concerns. Become familiar with these symbols so that when you see them, you will know what they mean and what to do. It is important that you read this entire safety section to learn about specific dangers in the laboratory.

If you are instructed to note the odor of a substance, wave the fumes toward your nose with your hand. Never put your nose close to the source.

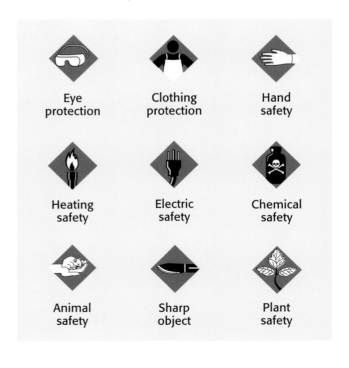

Eye protection

Clothing protection

Hand safety

Heating safety

Electric safety

Chemical safety

Animal safety

Sharp object

Plant safety

Eye Safety

Wear safety goggles when working around chemicals, acids, bases, or any type of flame or heating device. Wear safety goggles any time there is even the slightest chance that harm could come to your eyes. If any substance gets into your eyes, notify your teacher immediately, and flush your eyes with running water for at least 15 minutes. Treat any unknown chemical as if it were a dangerous chemical. Never look directly into the sun. Doing so could cause permanent blindness.

Avoid wearing contact lenses in a laboratory situation. Even if you are wearing safety goggles, chemicals can get between the contact lenses and your eyes. If your doctor requires that you wear contact lenses instead of glasses, wear eye-cup safety goggles in the lab.

Safety Equipment

Know the locations of the nearest fire alarms and any other safety equipment, such as fire blankets and eyewash fountains, as identified by your teacher, and know the procedures for using them.

Be extra careful when using any glassware. When adding a heavy object to a graduated cylinder, tilt the cylinder so the object slides slowly to the bottom.

Neatness

Keep your work area free of all unnecessary books and papers. Tie back long hair, and secure loose sleeves or other loose articles of clothing, such as ties and bows. Remove dangling jewelry. Don't wear open-toed shoes or sandals in the laboratory. Never eat, drink, or apply cosmetics in a laboratory setting. Food, drink, and cosmetics can easily become contaminated with dangerous materials.

Certain hair products (such as aerosol hair spray) are flammable and should not be worn while working near an open flame. Avoid wearing hair spray or hair gel on lab days.

Sharp/Pointed Objects

Use knives and other sharp instruments with extreme care. Never cut objects while holding them in your hands. Place objects on a suitable work surface for cutting.

Heat

Wear safety goggles when using a heating device or a flame. Whenever possible, use an electric hot plate as a heat source instead of an open flame. When heating materials in a test tube, always angle the test tube away from yourself and others. In order to avoid burns, wear heat-resistant gloves whenever instructed to do so.

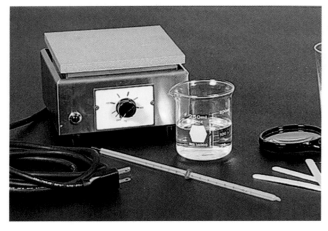

Electricity

Be careful with electrical cords. When using a microscope with a lamp, do not place the cord where it could trip someone. Do not let cords hang over a table edge in a way that could cause equipment to fall if the cord is accidentally pulled. Do not use equipment with damaged cords. Be sure your hands are dry and that the electrical equipment is in the "off" position before plugging it in. Turn off and unplug electrical equipment when you are finished.

Chemicals

Wear safety goggles when handling any potentially dangerous chemicals, acids, or bases. If a chemical is unknown, handle it as you would a dangerous chemical. Wear an apron and safety gloves when working with acids or bases or whenever you are told to do so. If a spill gets on your skin or clothing, rinse it off immediately with water for at least 5 minutes while calling to your teacher.

Never mix chemicals unless your teacher tells you to do so. Never taste, touch, or smell chemicals unless you are specifically directed to do so. Before working with a flammable liquid or gas, check for the presence of any source of flame, spark, or heat.

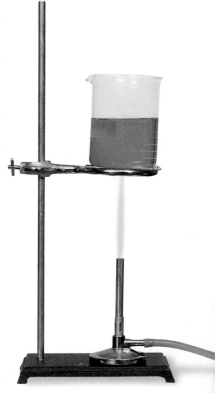

Animal Safety

Always obtain your teacher's permission before bringing any animal into the school building. Handle animals only as your teacher directs. Always treat animals carefully and with respect. Wash your hands thoroughly after handling any animal.

Plant Safety

Do not eat any part of a plant or plant seed used in the laboratory. Wash hands thoroughly after handling any part of a plant. When in nature, do not pick any wild plants unless your teacher instructs you to do so.

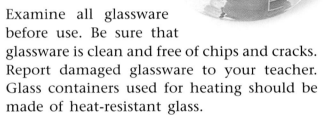

Glassware

Examine all glassware before use. Be sure that glassware is clean and free of chips and cracks. Report damaged glassware to your teacher. Glass containers used for heating should be made of heat-resistant glass.

**DESIGN
YOUR OWN**

Aunt Flossie and the Bumblebee

Materials

• to be determined by each experimental design and approved by the teacher

Last week Aunt Flossie came to watch the soccer game, and she was chased by a big yellow-and-black bumblebee. Everyone tried not to laugh, but Aunt Flossie did look pretty funny. She was running and screaming, all perfumed and dressed in a bright floral dress, shiny jewelry, and a huge hat with a big purple bow. No one could understand why the bumblebee tormented Aunt Flossie and left everyone else alone. She said that she would not come to another game until you determine why the bee chased her.

Your job is to design an experiment that will determine why the bee was attracted to Aunt Flossie. You may simulate the situation by using objects that contain the same sensory clues that Aunt Flossie wore that day—bright, shiny colors and strong scents.

Ask a Question

1. Use the information in the story above to help you form questions. Make a list of Aunt Flossie's characteristics on the day of the soccer game. What was Aunt Flossie wearing? What do you think she looked like to a bumblebee? What scent was she wearing? Which of those characteristics may have affected the bee's behavior? What was it about Aunt Flossie that affected the bee's behavior?

Form a Hypothesis

2. Write a hypothesis about insect behavior based on your observations of Aunt Flossie and the bumblebee at the soccer game. A possible hypothesis is, "Insects are attracted to strong floral scents." Write your own hypothesis.

Test the Hypothesis

3. Outline a procedure for your experiment. Be sure to follow the steps in the scientific method. Design your procedure to answer specific questions. For example, if you want to know if insects are attracted to different colors, you might want to display cutouts of several colors of paper.

4. Make a list of materials for your experiment. You may want to include colored paper, pictures from magazines, or strong perfumes as bait. You may not use living things as bait in your experiment. Your teacher must approve your experimental design before you begin.

5. Determine a place to conduct your experiment. For example, you may want to place your materials in a box on the ground, or you may want to hang items from a tree branch. **Caution:** Be sure to remain at a safe distance from your experimental setup. Do not touch any insects. Have an adult help you release any insects that are trapped or collected.

6. Develop data tables for recording the results of your trials. For example, a data table similar to the one at right may be used to record the results of testing different colors to see which insects are attracted to them. Design your data tables to fit your investigation.

Analyze the Results

7. Describe your experimental procedure. Did your results support your hypothesis? Explain.

8. Compare your results with those of your classmates. Which hypotheses were supported? What conclusions can you draw from the class results?

Communicate Results

9. Write a letter to Aunt Flossie telling her what you have learned. Tell her what caused the bee attack. Invite her to attend another soccer game, and advise her about what she should or should not wear!

Effects of Color

Color	Number of bees	Number of ants	Number of wasps
Red			
Blue			
Yellow			

DO NOT WRITE IN BOOK

The Cricket Caper

Insects are a special class of invertebrates with more than 750,000 known species. Insects may be the most successful group of animals on Earth. In this activity, you will observe a cricket's structure and the simple adaptive behaviors that help make it so successful. Remember, you will be handling a living animal that deserves to be treated with care.

Materials

- 2 crickets
- 600 mL beakers (2)
- plastic wrap
- apple
- hand lens (optional)
- masking tape
- aluminum foil
- lamp
- 2 sealable plastic bags
- crushed ice
- hot tap water

Procedure

1. Place a cricket in a clean 600 mL beaker. Quickly cover the beaker with plastic wrap.

2. Without much movement, observe the cricket's structure. Record your observations in your ScienceLog.

3. Place a small piece of apple in the beaker. Set the beaker on a table. Quietly observe the cricket for several minutes. (Any movement may cause the cricket to stop what it is doing.) Record your observations.

4. Remove the plastic wrap and the apple from the beaker, and quickly attach a second beaker. Join the two beakers together at the mouths with masking tape. Handle the beakers carefully. Remember, a living thing is inside.

5. Wrap one of the joined beakers with aluminum foil. Lay the joined beakers on their sides. If the cricket is not visible, gently tap the sides of the beaker until it is exposed.

6. Record the cricket's location. Shine a lamp on the uncovered side of the beaker. Record the cricket's location after 5 minutes.

7. Without disturbing the cricket, move the aluminum foil to the other beaker. Repeat step 6 to see if you get the same result.

8. Fill one sealable plastic bag halfway with crushed ice and seal it. Fill the other bag with hot tap water and seal it. Lay the bags side by side. Remove the foil from the joined beakers.

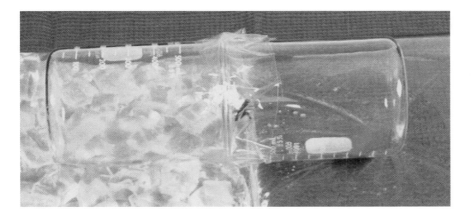

9. Gently rock the beakers until the cricket is in the center. Place the beakers on the plastic bags as shown. Observe the cricket's behavior for 5 minutes. Record your observations.

10. Set the beakers on one end for several minutes to allow them to return to room temperature. Repeat step 9 and 10 three times. (Why is it necessary to allow the beakers to return to room temperature each time?)

11. Set the beakers on end. Carefully remove the masking tape and separate the beakers. Quickly replace the plastic wrap on the beaker with the cricket.

12. Make a data table similar to the one shown. Observe the cricket's movement every 15 seconds for 3 minutes. Record data in the One Cricket column of the table using these codes: 0 = no movement, 1 = slight movement, 2 = rapid movement.

13. Place a second cricket (Cricket B) into the beaker with the first Cricket (Cricket A). Observe both crickets' behavior every 15 seconds. Record data using the codes in step 12.

Analysis

14. Describe the crickets' feeding behavior. Are they lappers, suckers, or chewers?

15. Do crickets prefer light or darkness? Explain.

16. From your observations, what can you infer about a cricket's temperature preferences?

17. Based on your observations of Cricket A and Cricket B, what general statements can you make about the social behavior of crickets?

	One Cricket	Two Crickets	
		A	B
15 s			
30 s			
45 s			
60 s			
75 s			
90 s		DO NOT WRITE IN BOOK	
105 s			
120 s			
135 s			
150 s			
165 s			
180 s			

A Prince of a Frog

Imagine that you are a scientist interested in amphibians. You have heard in the news about amphibians disappearing all over the world. What a great loss it will be to the environment if all amphibians become extinct! Your job is to learn as much as possible about how frogs normally behave so that you can act as a resource for other scientists who are studying the problem.

In this activity, you will observe a normal frog in a dry container and in water.

Materials

- live frog in a dry container
- live crickets
- 600 mL beaker
- container half-filled with dechlorinated water
- large rock (optional)
- protective gloves

Procedure

1. In your ScienceLog, make a table similar to the one below to note all of your observations of the frog in this investigation.

Observations of a Live Frog	
Characteristic	**Observation**
Breathing	
Eyes	
Legs	
Response to food	DO NOT WRITE IN BOOK
Skin texture	
Swimming behavior	
Skin coloration	

2. Observe a live frog in a dry container. Draw the frog in your ScienceLog. Label the eyes, nostrils, front legs, and hind legs.

3. Watch the frog's movements as it breathes air with its lungs. Write a description of the frog's breathing in your ScienceLog.

4. Look closely at the frog's eyes, and note their location. Examine the upper and lower eyelids as well as the transparent third eyelid. Which of these three eyelids actually moves over the eye?

5. Study the frog's legs. Note in your data table the difference between the front and hind legs.

6. Place a live insect, such as a cricket, in the container. Observe and record how the frog reacts.

7. Carefully pick up the frog, and examine its skin. How does it feel?
   Caution: Remember that a frog is a living thing and deserves to be handled gently and with respect.

8. Place a 600 mL beaker in the container. Place the frog in the beaker. Cover the beaker with your hand, and carry it to a container of dechlorinated water. Tilt the beaker and gently submerge it in the water until the frog swims out of the beaker.

9. Watch the frog float and swim in the water. How does the frog use its legs to swim? Notice the position of the frog's head.

10. As the frog swims, bend down and look up into the water so that you can see the underside of the frog. Then look down on the frog from above. Compare the color on the top and the underneath sides of the frog. Record your observations in your data table.

Analysis

11. From the position of the frog's eyes, what can you infer about the frog's field of vision? How might the position of the frog's eyes benefit the frog while it is swimming?

12. How can a frog "breathe" while it is swimming in water?

13. How are the hind legs of a frog adapted for life on land and in water?

14. What differences did you notice in coloration on the frog's top side and its underneath side? What advantage might these color differences provide?

15. How does the frog eat? What senses are involved in helping the frog catch its prey?

Going Further
Observe another type of amphibian, such as a salamander. How do the adaptations of other types of amphibians compare with those of the frog you observed in this investigation?

Concept Mapping: A Way to Bring Ideas Together

What Is a Concept Map?

Have you ever tried to tell someone about a book or a chapter you've just read and found that you can remember only a few isolated words and ideas? Or maybe you've memorized facts for a test and then weeks later discovered you're not even sure what topics those facts covered.

In both cases, you may have understood the ideas or concepts by themselves but not in relation to one another. If you could somehow link the ideas together, you would probably understand them better and remember them longer. This is something a concept map can help you do. A concept map is a way to see how ideas or concepts fit together. It can help you see the "big picture."

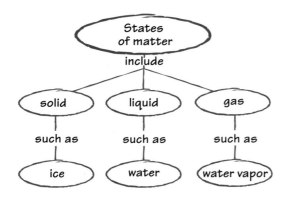

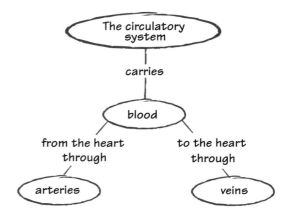

How to Make a Concept Map

❶ Make a list of the main ideas or concepts.

It might help to write each concept on its own slip of paper. This will make it easier to rearrange the concepts as many times as necessary to make sense of how the concepts are connected. After you've made a few concept maps this way, you can go directly from writing your list to actually making the map.

❷ Arrange the concepts in order from the most general to the most specific.

Put the most general concept at the top and circle it. Ask yourself, "How does this concept relate to the remaining concepts?" As you see the relationships, arrange the concepts in order from general to specific.

❸ Connect the related concepts with lines.

❹ On each line, write an action word or short phrase that shows how the concepts are related.

Look at the concept maps on this page, and then see if you can make one for the following terms:

plants, water, photosynthesis, carbon dioxide, sun's energy

One possible answer is provided at right, but don't look at it until you try the concept map yourself.

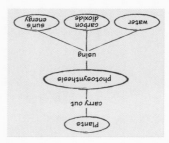

SI Measurement

The International System of Units, or SI, is the standard system of measurement used by many scientists. Using the same standards of measurement makes it easier for scientists to communicate with one another.

SI works by combining prefixes and base units. Each base unit can be used with different prefixes to define smaller and larger quantities. The table below lists common SI prefixes.

SI Prefixes			
Prefix	**Abbreviation**	**Factor**	**Example**
kilo-	k	1,000	kilogram, 1 kg = 1,000 g
hecto-	h	100	hectoliter, 1 hL = 100 L
deka-	da	10	dekameter, 1 dam = 10 m
		1	meter, liter
deci-	d	0.1	decigram, 1 dg = 0.1 g
centi-	c	0.01	centimeter, 1 cm = 0.01 m
milli-	m	0.001	milliliter, 1 mL = 0.001 L
micro-	μ	0.000 001	micrometer, 1 μm = 0.000 001 m

SI Conversion Table		
SI units	**From SI to English**	**From English to SI**
Length		
kilometer (km) = 1,000 m	1 km = 0.621 mi	1 mi = 1.609 km
meter (m) = 100 cm	1 m = 3.281 ft	1 ft = 0.305 m
centimeter (cm) = 0.01 m	1 cm = 0.394 in.	1 in. = 2.540 cm
millimeter (mm) = 0.001 m	1 mm = 0.039 in.	
micrometer (μm) = 0.000 001 m		
nanometer (nm) = 0.000 000 001 m		
Area		
square kilometer (km^2) = 100 hectares	1 km^2 = 0.386 mi^2	1 mi^2 = 2.590 km^2
hectare (ha) = 10,000 m^2	1 ha = 2.471 acres	1 acre = 0.405 ha
square meter (m^2) = 10,000 cm^2	1 m^2 = 10.765 ft^2	1 ft^2 = 0.093 m^2
square centimeter (cm^2) = 100 mm^2	1 cm^2 = 0.155 in.^{2}	1 in.^{2} = 6.452 cm^2
Volume		
liter (L) = 1,000 mL = 1 dm^3	1 L = 1.057 fl qt	1 fl qt = 0.946 L
milliliter (mL) = 0.001 L = 1 cm^3	1 mL = 0.034 fl oz	1 fl oz = 29.575 mL
microliter (μL) = 0.000 001 L		
Mass		
kilogram (kg) = 1,000 g	1 kg = 2.205 lb	1 lb = 0.454 kg
gram (g) = 1,000 mg	1 g = 0.035 oz	1 oz = 28.349 g
milligram (mg) = 0.001 g		
microgram (μg) = 0.000 001 g		

Temperature Scales

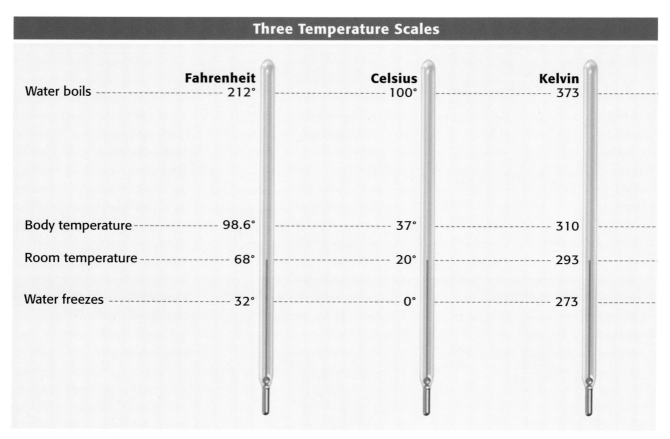

Temperature can be expressed using three different scales: Fahrenheit, Celsius, and Kelvin. The SI unit for temperature is the kelvin (K).

Although 0 K is much colder than 0°C, a change of 1 K is equal to a change of 1°C.

Three Temperature Scales

	Fahrenheit	Celsius	Kelvin
Water boils	212°	100°	373
Body temperature	98.6°	37°	310
Room temperature	68°	20°	293
Water freezes	32°	0°	273

Temperature Conversions Table

To convert	Use this equation:	Example
Celsius to Fahrenheit $°C \longrightarrow °F$	$°F = \left(\frac{9}{5} \times °C\right) + 32$	Convert 45°C to °F. $°F = \left(\frac{9}{5} \times 45°C\right) + 32 = 113°F$
Fahrenheit to Celsius $°F \longrightarrow °C$	$°C = \frac{5}{9} \times (°F - 32)$	Convert 68°F to °C. $°C = \frac{5}{9} \times (68°F - 32) = 20°C$
Celsius to Kelvin $°C \longrightarrow K$	$K = °C + 273$	Convert 45°C to K. $K = 45°C + 273 = 318 K$
Kelvin to Celsius $K \longrightarrow °C$	$°C = K - 273$	Convert 32 K to °C. $°C = 32 K - 273 = -241°C$

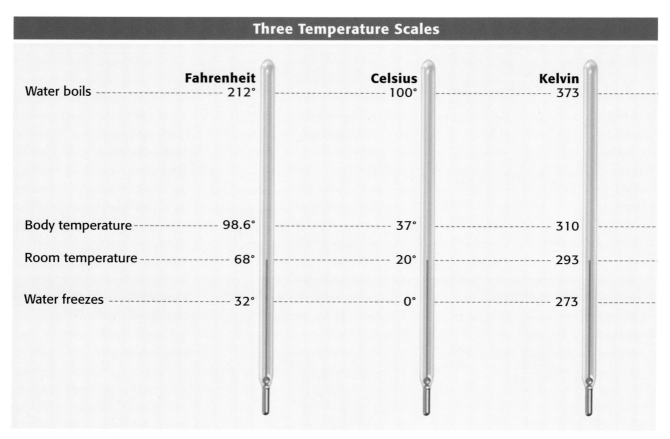

APPENDIX

Measuring Skills

Using a Graduated Cylinder

When using a graduated cylinder to measure volume, keep the following procedures in mind:

1 Make sure the cylinder is on a flat, level surface.

2 Move your head so that your eye is level with the surface of the liquid.

3 Read the mark closest to the liquid level. On glass graduated cylinders, read the mark closest to the center of the curve in the liquid's surface.

Using a Meterstick or Metric Ruler

When using a meterstick or metric ruler to measure length, keep the following procedures in mind:

1 Place the ruler firmly against the object you are measuring.

2 Align one edge of the object exactly with the zero end of the ruler.

3 Look at the other edge of the object to see which of the marks on the ruler is closest to that edge. **Note:** Each small slash between the centimeters represents a millimeter, which is one-tenth of a centimeter.

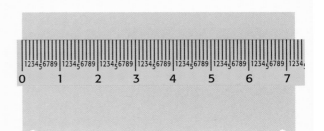

Using a Triple-Beam Balance

When using a triple-beam balance to measure mass, keep the following procedures in mind:

1 Make sure the balance is on a level surface.

2 Place all of the countermasses at zero. Adjust the balancing knob until the pointer rests at zero.

3 Place the object you wish to measure on the pan. **Caution:** Do not place hot objects or chemicals directly on the balance pan.

4 Move the largest countermass along the beam to the right until it is at the last notch that does not tip the balance. Follow the same procedure with the next-largest countermass. Then move the smallest countermass until the pointer rests at zero.

5 Add the readings from the three beams together to determine the mass of the object.

6 When determining the mass of crystals or powders, use a piece of filter paper. First find the mass of the paper. Then add the crystals or powder to the paper and re-measure. The actual mass of the crystals or powder is the total mass minus the mass of the paper. When finding the mass of liquids, first find the mass of the empty container. Then find the mass of the liquid and container together. The mass of the liquid is the total mass minus the mass of the container.

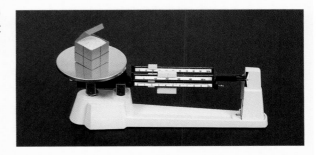

Scientific Method

The series of steps that scientists use to answer questions and solve problems is often called the **scientific method.** The scientific method is not a rigid procedure. Scientists may use all of the steps or just some of the steps of the scientific method. They may even repeat some of the steps. The goal of the scientific method is to come up with reliable answers and solutions.

Six Steps of the Scientific Method

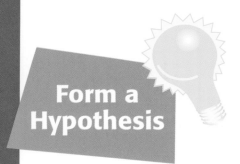

1 **Ask a Question** Good questions come from careful **observations.** You make observations by using your senses to gather information. Sometimes you may use instruments, such as microscopes and telescopes, to extend the range of your senses. As you observe the natural world, you will discover that you have many more questions than answers. These questions drive the scientific method.

Questions beginning with *what, why, how,* and *when* are very important in focusing an investigation, and they often lead to a hypothesis. (You will learn what a hypothesis is in the next step.) Here is an example of a question that could lead to further investigation.

Question: How does acid rain affect plant growth?

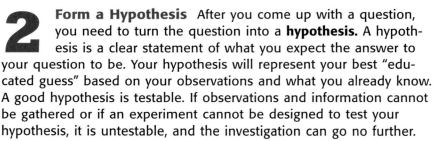

2 **Form a Hypothesis** After you come up with a question, you need to turn the question into a **hypothesis.** A hypothesis is a clear statement of what you expect the answer to your question to be. Your hypothesis will represent your best "educated guess" based on your observations and what you already know. A good hypothesis is testable. If observations and information cannot be gathered or if an experiment cannot be designed to test your hypothesis, it is untestable, and the investigation can go no further.

Here is a hypothesis that could be formed from the question, "How does acid rain affect plant growth?"

Hypothesis: Acid rain causes plants to grow more slowly.

Notice that the hypothesis provides some specifics that lead to methods of testing. The hypothesis can also lead to predictions. A **prediction** is what you think will be the outcome of your experiment or data collection. Predictions are usually stated in an "if . . . then" format. For example, **if** meat is kept at room temperature, **then** it will spoil faster than meat kept in the refrigerator. More than one prediction can be made for a single hypothesis. Here is a sample prediction for the hypothesis that acid rain causes plants to grow more slowly.

Prediction: If a plant is watered with only acid rain (which has a pH of 4), then the plant will grow at half its normal rate.

3 **Test the Hypothesis** After you have formed a hypothesis and made a prediction, you should test your hypothesis. There are different ways to do this. Perhaps the most familiar way is to conduct a **controlled experiment.** A controlled experiment tests only one factor at a time. A controlled experiment has a **control group** and one or more **experimental groups.** All the factors for the control and experimental groups are the same except for one factor, which is called the **variable.** By changing only one factor, you can see the results of just that one change.

Sometimes, the nature of an investigation makes a controlled experiment impossible. For example, dinosaurs have been extinct for millions of years, and the Earth's core is surrounded by thousands of meters of rock. It would be difficult, if not impossible, to conduct controlled experiments on such things. Under such circumstances, a hypothesis may be tested by making detailed observations. Taking measurements is one way of making observations.

Test the Hypothesis

4 **Analyze the Results** After you have completed your experiments, made your observations, and collected your data, you must analyze all the information you have gathered. Tables and graphs are often used in this step to organize the data.

Analyze the Results

5 **Draw Conclusions** Based on the analysis of your data, you should conclude whether or not your results support your hypothesis. If your hypothesis is supported, you (or others) might want to repeat the observations or experiments to verify your results. If your hypothesis is not supported by the data, you may have to check your procedure for errors. You may even have to reject your hypothesis and make a new one. If you cannot draw a conclusion from your results, you may have to try the investigation again or carry out further observations or experiments.

Draw Conclusions

Do they support your hypothesis?

No

Yes

6 **Communicate Results** After any scientific investigation, you should report your results. By doing a written or oral report, you let others know what you have learned. They may want to repeat your investigation to see if they get the same results. Your report may even lead to another question, which in turn may lead to another investigation.

Communicate Results

Scientific Method in Action

The scientific method is not a "straight line" of steps. It contains loops in which several steps may be repeated over and over again, while others may not be necessary. For example, sometimes scientists will find that testing one hypothesis raises new questions and new hypotheses to be tested. And sometimes, testing the hypothesis leads directly to a conclusion. Furthermore, the steps in the scientific method are not always used in the same order. Follow the steps in the diagram below, and see how many different directions the scientific method can take you.

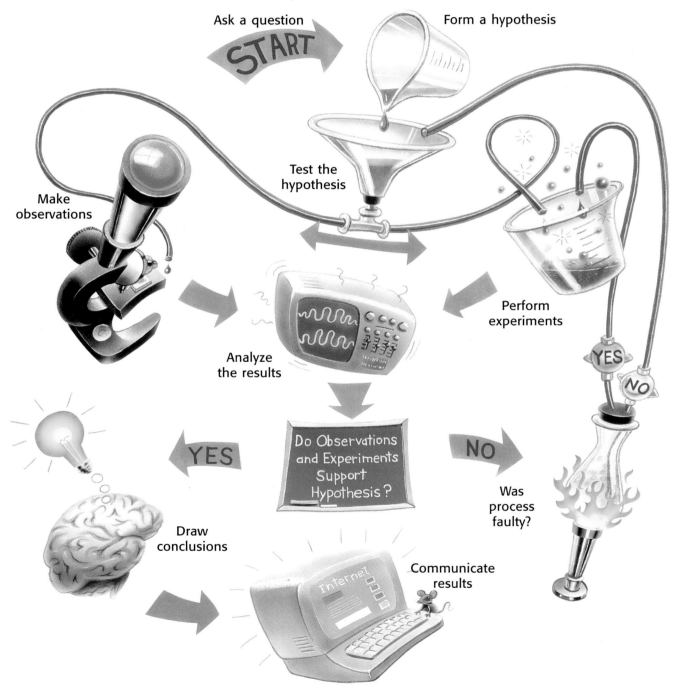

Ask a question

START

Form a hypothesis

Make observations

Test the hypothesis

Perform experiments

Analyze the results

Do Observations and Experiments Support Hypothesis?

YES

NO

Was process faulty?

Draw conclusions

Communicate results

Internet

Making Charts and Graphs

Circle Graphs

A circle graph, or pie chart, shows how each group of data relates to all of the data. Each part of the circle represents a category of the data. The entire circle represents all of the data. For example, a biologist studying a hardwood forest in Wisconsin found that there were five different types of trees. The data table at right summarizes the biologist's findings.

Wisconsin Hardwood Trees	
Type of tree	**Number found**
Oak	600
Maple	750
Beech	300
Birch	1,200
Hickory	150
Total	3,000

How to Make a Circle Graph

1 In order to make a circle graph of this data, first find the percentage of each type of tree. To do this, divide the number of individual trees by the total number of trees and multiply by 100.

$$\frac{600 \text{ oak}}{3,000 \text{ trees}} \times 100 = 20\%$$

$$\frac{750 \text{ maple}}{3,000 \text{ trees}} \times 100 = 25\%$$

$$\frac{300 \text{ beech}}{3,000 \text{ trees}} \times 100 = 10\%$$

$$\frac{1,200 \text{ birch}}{3,000 \text{ trees}} \times 100 = 40\%$$

$$\frac{150 \text{ hickory}}{3,000 \text{ trees}} \times 100 = 5\%$$

2 Now determine the size of the pie shapes that make up the chart. Do this by multiplying each percentage by 360°. Remember that a circle contains 360°.

20% × 360° = 72°	25% × 360° = 90°
10% × 360° = 36°	40% × 360° = 144°
5% × 360° = 18°	

3 Then check that the sum of the percentages is 100 and the sum of the degrees is 360.

20% + 25% + 10% + 40% + 5% = 100%

72° + 90° + 36° + 144° + 18° = 360°

4 Use a compass to draw a circle and mark its center.

5 Then use a protractor to draw angles of 72°, 90°, 36°, 144°, and 18° in the circle.

6 Finally, label each part of the graph, and choose an appropriate title.

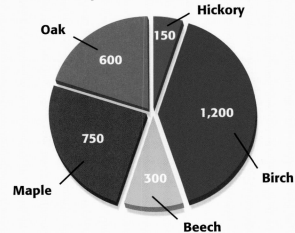

A Community of Wisconsin Hardwood Trees

Population of Appleton, 1900–2000	
Year	Population
1900	1,800
1920	2,500
1940	3,200
1960	3,900
1980	4,600
2000	5,300

Line Graphs

Line graphs are most often used to demonstrate continuous change. For example, Mr. Smith's science class analyzed the population records for their hometown, Appleton, between 1900 and 2000. Examine the data at left.

Because the year and the population change, they are the *variables*. The population is determined by, or dependent on, the year. Therefore, the population is called the **dependent variable**, and the year is called the **independent variable**. Each set of data is called a **data pair**. To prepare a line graph, data pairs must first be organized in a table like the one at left.

How to Make a Line Graph

1 Place the independent variable along the horizontal (*x*) axis. Place the dependent variable along the vertical (*y*) axis.

2 Label the *x*-axis "Year" and the *y*-axis "Population." Look at your largest and smallest values for the population. Determine a scale for the *y*-axis that will provide enough space to show these values. You must use the same scale for the entire length of the axis. Find an appropriate scale for the *x*-axis too.

3 Choose reasonable starting points for each axis.

4 Plot the data pairs as accurately as possible.

5 Choose a title that accurately represents the data.

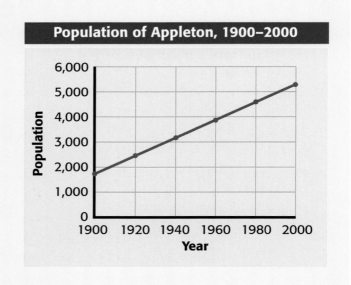

How to Determine Slope

Slope is the ratio of the change in the *y*-axis to the change in the *x*-axis, or "rise over run."

1 Choose two points on the line graph. For example, the population of Appleton in 2000 was 5,300 people. Therefore, you can define point *a* as (2000, 5,300). In 1900, the population was 1,800 people. Define point *b* as (1900, 1,800).

2 Find the change in the *y*-axis.
(*y* at point *a*) − (*y* at point *b*)
5,300 people − 1,800 people = 3,500 people

3 Find the change in the *x*-axis.
(*x* at point *a*) − (*x* at point *b*)
2000 − 1900 = 100 years

4 Calculate the slope of the graph by dividing the change in *y* by the change in *x*.

$$\text{slope} = \frac{\text{change in } y}{\text{change in } x}$$

$$\text{slope} = \frac{3,500 \text{ people}}{100 \text{ years}}$$

slope = 35 people per year

In this example, the population in Appleton increased by a fixed amount each year. The graph of this data is a straight line. Therefore, the relationship is **linear.** When the graph of a set of data is not a straight line, the relationship is **nonlinear.**

Using Algebra to Determine Slope

The equation in step 4 may also be arranged to be:

$$y = kx$$

where y represents the change in the y-axis, k represents the slope, and x represents the change in the x-axis.

$$\text{slope} = \frac{\text{change in } y}{\text{change in } x}$$

$$k = \frac{y}{x}$$

$$k \times x = \frac{y \times x}{x}$$

$$kx = y$$

Bar Graphs

Bar graphs are used to demonstrate change that is not continuous. These graphs can be used to indicate trends when the data are taken over a long period of time. A meteorologist gathered the precipitation records at right for Hartford, Connecticut, for April 1–15, 1996, and used a bar graph to represent the data.

Precipitation in Hartford, Connecticut April 1–15, 1996

Date	Precipitation (cm)	Date	Precipitation (cm)
April 1	0.5	April 9	0.25
April 2	1.25	April 10	0.0
April 3	0.0	April 11	1.0
April 4	0.0	April 12	0.0
April 5	0.0	April 13	0.25
April 6	0.0	April 14	0.0
April 7	0.0	April 15	6.50
April 8	1.75		

How to Make a Bar Graph

1. Use an appropriate scale and a reasonable starting point for each axis.
2. Label the axes, and plot the data.
3. Choose a title that accurately represents the data.

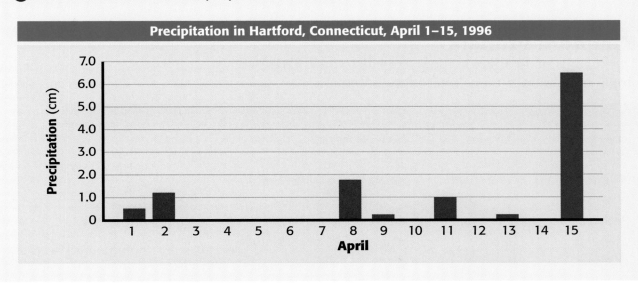

The Six Kingdoms

Kingdom Archaebacteria

The organisms in this kingdom are single-celled prokaryotes.

Archaebacteria		
Group	**Examples**	**Characteristics**
Methanogens	*Methanococcus*	found in soil, swamps, the digestive tract of mammals; produce methane gas; can't live in oxygen
Thermophiles	*Sulpholobus*	found in extremely hot environments; require sulphur, can't live in oxygen
Halophiles	*Halococcus*	found in environments with very high salt content, such as the Dead Sea; nearly all can live in oxygen

Kingdom Eubacteria

There are more than 4,000 named species in this kingdom of single-celled prokaryotes.

Eubacteria		
Group	**Examples**	**Characteristics**
Bacilli	*Escherichia coli*	rod-shaped; free-living, symbiotic, or parasitic; some can fix nitrogen; some cause disease
Cocci	*Streptococcus*	spherical-shaped, disease-causing; can form spores to resist unfavorable environments
Spirilla	*Treponema*	spiral-shaped; responsible for several serious illnesses, such as syphilis and Lyme disease

Kingdom Protista

The organisms in this kingdom are eukaryotes. There are single-celled and multicellular representatives.

Protists		
Group	**Examples**	**Characteristics**
Sacodines	*Amoeba*	radiolarians; single-celled consumers
Ciliates	*Paramecium*	single-celled consumers
Flagellates	*Trypanosoma*	single-celled parasites
Sporozoans	*Plasmodium*	single-celled parasites
Euglenas	*Euglena*	single-celled; photosynthesize
Diatoms	*Pinnularia*	most are single-celled; photosynthesize
Dinoflagellates	*Gymnodinium*	single-celled; some photosynthesize
Algae	*Volvox,* coral algae	4 phyla; single- or many-celled; photosynthesize
Slime molds	*Physarum*	single- or many-celled; consumers or decomposers
Water molds	powdery mildew	single- or many-celled, parasites or decomposers

Kingdom Fungi

There are single-celled and multicellular eukaryotes in this kingdom. There are four major groups of fungi.

Fungi		
Group	**Examples**	**Characteristics**
Threadlike fungi	bread mold	spherical; decomposers
Sac fungi	yeast, morels	saclike; parasites and decomposers
Club fungi	mushrooms, rusts, smuts	club-shaped; parasites and decomposers
Lichens	British soldier	symbiotic with algae

Kingdom Plantae

The organisms in this kingdom are multicellular eukaryotes. They have specialized organ systems for different life processes. They are classified in divisions instead of phyla.

Plants		
Group	**Examples**	**Characteristics**
Bryophytes	mosses, liverworts	reproduce by spores
Club mosses	*Lycopodium,* ground pine	reproduce by spores
Horsetails	rushes	reproduce by spores
Ferns	spleenworts, sensitive fern	reproduce by spores
Conifers	pines, spruces, firs	reproduce by seeds; cones
Cycads	*Zamia*	reproduce by seeds
Gnetophytes	*Welwitschia*	reproduce by seeds
Ginkgoes	*Ginkgo*	reproduce by seeds
Angiosperms	all flowering plants	reproduce by seeds; flowers

Kingdom Animalia

This kingdom contains multicellular eukaryotes. They have specialized tissues and complex organ systems.

Animals		
Group	**Examples**	**Characteristics**
Sponges	glass sponges	no symmetry or segmentation; aquatic
Cnidarians	jellyfish, coral	radial symmetry; aquatic
Flatworms	planaria, tapeworms, flukes	bilateral symmetry; organ systems
Roundworms	*Trichina,* hookworms	bilateral symmetry; organ systems
Annelids	earthworms, leeches	bilateral symmetry; organ systems
Mollusks	snails, octopuses	bilateral symmetry; organ systems
Echinoderms	sea stars, sand dollars	radial symmetry; organ systems
Arthropods	insects, spiders, lobsters	bilateral symmetry; organ systems
Chordates	fish, amphibians, reptiles, birds, mammals	bilateral symmetry; complex organ systems

Using the Microscope

Parts of the Compound Light Microscope

- The **ocular lens** magnifies the image 10×.
- The **low-power objective** magnifies the image 10×.
- The **high-power objective** magnifies the image either 40× or 43×.
- The **revolving nosepiece** holds the objectives and can be turned to change from one magnification to the other.
- The **body tube** maintains the correct distance between the ocular lens and objectives.
- The **coarse-adjustment knob** moves the body tube up and down to allow focusing of the image.

- The **fine-adjustment knob** moves the body tube slightly to bring the image into sharper focus.
- The **stage** supports a slide.
- **Stage clips** hold the slide in place for viewing.
- The **diaphragm** controls the amount of light coming through the stage.
- The light source provides a **light** for viewing the slide.
- The **arm** supports the body tube.
- The **base** supports the microscope.

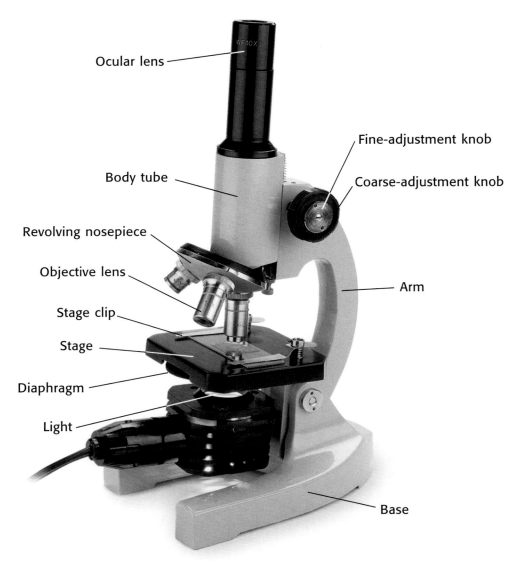

Ocular lens

Fine-adjustment knob

Body tube

Coarse-adjustment knob

Revolving nosepiece

Objective lens

Arm

Stage clip

Stage

Diaphragm

Light

Base

Proper Use of the Compound Light Microscope

1 Carry the microscope to your lab table using both hands. Place one hand beneath the base, and use the other hand to hold the arm of the microscope. Hold the microscope close to your body while moving it to your lab table.

2 Place the microscope on the lab table at least 5 cm from the edge of the table.

3 Check to see what type of light source is used by your microscope. If the microscope has a lamp, plug it in, making sure that the cord is out of the way. If the microscope has a mirror, adjust it to reflect light through the hole in the stage.
Caution: If your microscope has a mirror, do not use direct sunlight as a light source. Direct sunlight can damage your eyes.

4 Always begin work with the low-power objective in line with the body tube. Adjust the revolving nosepiece.

5 Place a prepared slide over the hole in the stage. Secure the slide with the stage clips.

6 Look through the ocular lens. Move the diaphragm to adjust the amount of light coming through the stage.

7 Look at the stage from eye level. Slowly turn the coarse adjustment to lower the objective until it almost touches the slide. Do not allow the objective to touch the slide.

8 Look through the ocular lens. Turn the coarse adjustment to raise the low-power objective until the image is in focus. Always focus by raising the objective away from the slide. *Never focus the objective downward.* Use the fine adjustment to sharpen the focus. Keep both eyes open while viewing a slide.

9 Make sure that the image is exactly in the center of your field of vision. Then switch to the high-power objective. Focus the image, using only the fine adjustment. *Never use the coarse adjustment at high power.*

10 When you are finished using the microscope, remove the slide. Clean the ocular lens and objective lenses with lens paper. Return the microscope to its storage area. Remember, you should use both hands to carry the microscope.

Making a Wet Mount

1 Use lens paper to clean a glass slide and a coverslip.

2 Place the specimen you wish to observe in the center of the slide.

3 Using a medicine dropper, place one drop of water on the specimen.

4 Hold the coverslip at the edge of the water and at a 45° angle to the slide. Make sure that the water runs along the edge of the coverslip.

5 Lower the coverslip slowly to avoid trapping air bubbles.

6 Water might evaporate from the slide as you work. Add more water to keep the specimen fresh. Place the tip of the medicine dropper next to the edge of the coverslip. Add a drop of water. (You can also use this method to add stain or solutions to a wet mount.) Remove excess water from the slide by using the corner of a paper towel as a blotter. Do not lift the coverslip to add or remove water.

Glossary

GLOSSARY

A

abdomen   the body part of an animal that usually contains the gut and other digestive organs (41)

altricial chick   (al TRISH uhl) a chick that hatches weak, naked, and helpless (94)

amniotic egg   (AM nee AH tik) an egg containing amniotic fluid to protect the developing embryo; usually surrounded by a hard shell (88)

amphibian   a type of vertebrate ectotherm that usually begins life in the water with gills and later develops lungs (68)

antennae   feelers on an arthropod's head that respond to touch, taste, or smell (42)

Archaebacteria   (AHR kee bak TIR ee uh) a classification kingdom containing bacteria that thrive in extreme environments (140)

asymmetrical   without symmetry (28)

B

bilateral symmetry   a body plan in which two halves of an organism's body are mirror images of each other (28)

biological clock   an internal control of natural cycles (12)

brain   the mass of nerve tissue that is the main organ of the nervous system (29)

brooding   when a bird sits on its eggs until they hatch (93)

C

camouflage   the coloration and/or texture that enables an animal to blend in with its environment (9)

carnivore   a consumer that eats animals (107)

cartilage   a flexible tissue that gives support and protection but is not rigid like bone (61, 65)

cell wall   a structure that surrounds the cell membrane of some cells and provides strength and support to the cell membrane (5)

cephalothorax   (SEF uh loh THOR aks) the body part of arachnids that consists of both a head and a thorax and that usually has four pairs of legs attached (43)

circadian rhythm   a natural, daily cycle (12)

closed circulatory system   a circulatory system in which a heart circulates blood through a network of vessels that forms a closed loop (38)

coelom   (SEE luhm) a cavity in the body of some animals where the gut and organs are located (29)

communication   a transfer of a signal from one animal to another that results in some type of response (14)

compound eye   an eye that is made of many identical, light-sensitive cells that work together (42)

compound light microscope   a microscope that consists of a tube with lenses, a stage, and a light source (142)

consumer   an organism that eats producers or other organisms for energy (7)

contour feather   a feather made of a stiff, central shaft with many side branches called barbs (89)

controlled experiment   an experiment that tests only one factor at a time (135)

D

denticles   small, sharp, toothlike structures on the skin of cartilaginous fishes (66)

diaphragm   (DIE uh FRAM) the sheet of muscle underneath the lungs of mammals that helps draw air into the lungs (101)

down feather   a fluffy, insulating feather that lies next to a bird's body (89)

E

ectotherm   an animal whose body temperature fluctuates with the environment's temperature (62)

embryo   an organism in the earliest stage of development (6)

endoskeleton   an internal skeleton (47)

endotherm   an animal that maintains a constant body temperature despite temperature changes in its environment (62)

estivation   a period of reduced activity that some animals experience in the summer (11)

Eubacteria   (YOO bak TIR ee uh) a classification kingdom containing mostly free-living bacteria found in many varied environments (140)

exoskeleton   an external skeleton made of protein and chitin; found on arthropods (42)

external fertilization   the fertilization of eggs by sperm that occurs outside the body of the female (64)

F

fins   fanlike structures that help fish move, turn, stop, and balance (64)

Fungi   a kingdom of complex organisms that obtain food by breaking down other substances in their surroundings and absorbing the nutrients (141)

G

ganglia groups of nerve cells (29)

gestation period (jeh STAY shuhn) the time during which an embryo develops within the mother (104)

gills organs that remove oxygen from the water and carbon dioxide from the blood (64)

gut the pouch where food is digested in animals (29)

H

head the body part of animals where the brain is located (41)

hibernation a period of inactivity that some animals experience in winter that allows them to survive on stored body fat (11)

host an organism on which a parasite lives (34)

hypothesis a possible explanation or answer to a question (134)

I

innate behavior a behavior that is influenced by genes and does not depend on learning (10)

internal fertilization the fertilization of an egg by sperm that occurs inside the body of a female (64)

invertebrate an animal without a backbone (5, 28)

L

landmark a fixed object used to determine location during navigation (13)

lateral line system a row or rows of tiny sense organs along the sides of a fish's body (64)

learned behavior a behavior that has been learned from experience or observation (10)

lift an upward force on an object caused by differences in pressure above and below the object; lift opposes the downward pull of gravity (92)

lung a saclike organ that takes oxygen from the air and delivers it to the blood (68)

M

mammary glands glands that secrete a nutritious fluid called milk (99)

mandible a jaw found on some arthropods (43)

marsupial a mammal that gives birth to live, partially developed young that continue to develop inside the mother's pouch or skin fold (103)

medusa a body form of some cnidarians; resembles a mushroom with tentacles (32)

metamorphosis the process in which an insect or other animal changes form as it develops from an embryo or larva to an adult (45, 70)

migrate to travel from one place to another in response to the seasons or environmental conditions (11)

monotreme a mammal that lays eggs (102)

multicellular made of many cells (5)

O

open circulatory system a circulatory system consisting of a heart that pumps blood through spaces called sinuses (38)

organ a combination of two or more tissues that work together to perform a specific function in the body (6)

P

parasite an organism that feeds on another living creature, usually without killing it (34)

pheromone (FER uh MON) a chemical produced by animals for communication (15)

placenta a special organ of exchange that provides a developing fetus with nutrients and oxygen (104)

placental mammal a mammal that nourishes its unborn offspring with a placenta inside the uterus and gives birth to well-developed young (104)

polyp a body form of some cnidarians; resembles a vase (32)

precocial chick (pree KOH shuhl) a chick that leaves the nest immediately after hatching and is fully active (94)

predator an organism that eats other organisms (8)

preening the activity in which a bird uses its beak to spread oil on its feathers (89)

prey an organism that is eaten by another organism (8)

primate a type of mammal that includes humans, apes, and monkeys; typically distinguished by opposable thumbs and binocular vision (111)

Protista a kingdom of eukaryotic single-celled or simple, multicellular organisms; kingdom Protista contains all eukaryotes that are not plants, animals, or fungi (140)

R

radial symmetry a body plan in which the parts of the body are arranged in a circle around a central point (28)

S

scales bony structures that cover the skin of bony fishes (66)

scientific method a series of steps that scientists use to answer questions and solve problems (134)

segment   one of many identical or almost identical repeating body parts (39)

sexual reproduction   reproduction in which two sex cells join to form a zygote; sexual reproduction produces offspring that share characteristics of both parents (6)

social behavior   the interaction between animals of the same species (14)

swim bladder   a balloonlike organ that is filled with oxygen and other gases; gives bony fish their buoyancy (66)

T

tadpole   the aquatic larvae of an amphibian (70)

territory   an area occupied by one animal or a group of animals from which other members of the species are excluded (14)

therapsid   (thuh RAP sid) a prehistoric reptile ancestor of mammals (73, 98)

thorax   the central body part of an arthropod or other animal; where the heart and lungs are located (41)

tissue   a group of similar cells that work together to perform a specific job in the body (6)

V

variable   a factor in a controlled experiment that changes (135)

vertebrae   (VUHR tuh BRAY) segments of bone or cartilage that interlock to form a backbone (61)

vertebrate   an animal with a skull and a backbone; includes mammals, birds, reptiles, amphibians, and fish (4, 60)

W

water vascular system   a system of water pumps and canals found in all echinoderms that allows them to move, eat, and breathe (48)

Index

INDEX

Credits

Abbreviations used: (t) top, (c) center, (b) bottom, (l) left, (r) right, (bkgd) background

ILLUSTRATIONS

All illustrations, unless otherwise noted below by Holt, Rinehart and Winston.

Chapter One Page 5 (chart), Sidney Jablonski; 5 (ant, beetle, bug, fish, mollusk, sponge, starfish, worm), Barbara Hoopes-Ambler; 5 (jellyfish), Sarah Woodward/Morgan-Cain & Associates; 5 (spider, fly), Steve Roberts; 5 (butterfly), Bridgette James; 5 (elephant), Michael Woods/Morgan-Cain & Associates; 6 (bl), Kip Carter; 10 (cl), Keith Locke/Suzanne Craig Represents Inc.; 12 (tr), Gary Locke/Suzanne Craig Represents Inc.; 12 (bl), Tony Morse/Ivy Glick; 16 (b), John White/The Neis Group; 20 (br), John White/The Neis Group; 23 (bl), Sidney Jablonski.

Chapter Two Page 29 (tl), Barbara Hoopes-Ambler; 29 (tc), Sarah Woodward/Morgan-Cain & Associates; 29 (tr), Alexander & Turner; 29 (cr,br), Alexander & Turner; 31, Alexander & Turner; 32, John White/The Neis Group; 33, Morgan-Cain & Associates; 34, Alexander & Turner; 37 (tr), Alexander & Turner; 41, Felipe Passalacqua; 43 (c), John White/The Neis Group; 43 (cr), Will Nelson/Sweet Reps; 45, Steve Roberts; 46, Bridgette James; 48 (tl), Alexander & Turner ; 48 (b), Alexander & Turner ; 55 (cr), Barbara Hoopes-Ambler.

Chapter Three Page 61 (t), Alexander & Turner ; 64 (cl), Will Nelson/Sweet Reps; 66 (br), Kip Carter; 66 (b), Barbara Hoopes-Ambler; 68 (br), Peg Gerrity; 70 (c), Will Nelson/Sweet Reps; 73 (c), Barbara Hoopes-Ambler; 75 (c), Kip Carter; 82 (bl), Will Nelson/Sweet Reps; 83 (bl), Marty Roper/Planet Rep; 83 (tr), Rob Schuster/Hankins and Tegenborg; 84 (bc), Ron Kimball; 85 (bl), Ka Botz.

Chapter Four Page 89 (feather), Will Nelson/Sweet Reps; 89 (bird), Will Nelson/Sweet Reps; 89 (closeup), Kip Carter; 89 (digestive system), Kip Carter; 90 (c), Will Nelson/Sweet Reps; 91, Will Nelson/Sweet Reps; 92 (c), Will Nelson/Sweet Reps; 97 (br), Kip Carter; 98 (bl), Howard Freidman; 112 (cr), Will Nelson/Sweet Reps; 115 (c), Yuan Lee; 117 (tr), Sidney Jablonski.

LabBook Page 124 (br), Keith Locke/Suzanne Craig Represents Inc.; 125 (tr), John White/The Neis Group; 126 (br) Marty Roper/Planet Rep.

Appendix Page 132 (t), Terry Guyer; 136 (b).

PHOTOGRAPHY

Cover and Title page: John Cancalosi/Peter Arnold, Inc.

Table of Contents v(tr), Zig Leszczynski/Animals Animals; v(cr), Lee Foster/FPG International; v(b), Peter Van Steen/HRW Photo; vi(tl), C. K. Lorenz/Photo Researchers, Inc.; vi(tcl), Gail Shumway/FPG International; vi(bcl), SuperStock; vi(bl), Leroy Simon/Visuals Unlimited; vii(tr), Frans Lanting/Minden Pictures; vii(cr), George D. Lepp/Stone; vii(br), Scott Daniel Peterson/Liaison.

Feature Borders: Unless otherwise noted below, all images copyright ©2001 PhotoDisc/HRW. "Across the Sciences" 84, 118, all images by HRW; "Eye on the Environment", 24, clouds and sea in bkgd, HRW; bkgd grass, red eyed frog, Corbis Images; hawks, pelican, Animals Animals/Earth Scenes; rat, Visuals Unlimited/John Grelach; endangered flower, Dan Suzio/Photo Researchers, Inc.; "Weird Science", 25, 56, 57, 85, 119, mite, David Burder/Stone; atom balls, J/B Woolsey Associates; walking stick, turtle, EclectiCollection.

Table of Contents: v(br), Uniphoto; vi(tl), Leonard Lessin/Photo Researchers, Inc.; vii(bl), Visuals Unlimited/R. Calentine; vii(tr), Robert Brons/BPS/Stone; viii(tr), Frans Lanting/Minden Pictures; viii(br), Biophoto Associates/Photo Researchers, Inc.; ix Centre National de Prehistoire, Perigueux, France; x(tl), G. Randall/FPG Int'l; x(bl), Fran Heyl Associates; xi(bl), SuperStock; xi(br), Phil Degginger; xii(bl), Richard R. Hansen/Photo Researchers, Inc.; xiii(tl), Daniel Schaefer/HRW Photo; xiii(br), Visuals Unlimited/James Beverigde; xiii(bl), Brian Parker/Tom Stack; xiii(tr), Carl Roessler/FPG Int'l; xiv(cr), Edwin & Peggy Bauer/Bruce Coleman; xiv(tl), Tui De Roy/Minden Pictures; xv(tl), Stuart Westmorland/Stone; xvii(tc), Dr. Dennis Kunkel/Phototake, Inc.; xvii(br), Image Bank; xviii(bl), Lennart Nilsson/Albert Bonniers Forlag AB, A CHILD IS BORN

Chapter One: p. 2-3 Bruce Coleman, Ltd./Natural Selection; 3 HRW Photo; James L. Amos/Peter Arnold; 4(b), David B. Fleetham/FPG Int'l; 6(tl), David M. Phillips/Photo Researchers, Inc.; 6(c), Visuals Unlimited/Fred Hossler; 7(tl), Gerard Lacz/Peter Arnold; 7(cr), Manoj Shah/Stone; 7(tr), Stephen Dalton/ Photo Researchers, Inc.; 7(br), Stephen Dalton/Photo Researchers, Inc.; 8 Tim Davis/Stone; 9(tr), J.H. Robinson/Photo Researchers, Inc.; 9(bl), W. Peckover/ Academy of Natural Sciences Philadelphia/VIREO; 9(br), Visuals Unlimited/Leroy Simon; 10(bl), Visuals Unlimited/A.J. Copley; 11(tr), George D. Lepp/Stone; 11(bl), Michio Hoshino/Minden Pictures; 13(t), FPG Int'l; 14(cl), Fernandez & Peck/Adventure Photo & Film; 14(bl), Peter Weimann/ Animals Animals; 15(tr), Lee F. Snyder/Photo Researchers, Inc.; 15(br), Johnny Johnson/Animals Animals; 16(tl), Ron Kimball; 17(tr), Planet Earth Pictures; 17(cr), Richard R. Hansen/Photo Researchers, Inc.; 20(c), Keren Su/Stone; 20(tr), Stephen Dalton/Photo Researchers, Inc.; 21 Lee F. Snyder/Photo Researchers, Inc.; 22 Visuals Unlimited/Leroy Simon; 24 John Elk/Stone; 25 Wayne Lawler/AUSCAPE

Chapter Two: p. 26-27 W. Gregory Brown/Animals Animals; 27 HRW Photo; 28(tr), SuperStock; 28(cl), Carl Roessler/FPG Int'l; 28(c), J Carmichael/ Image Bank; 28(bl), David B. Fleetham/Tom Stack; 30(cl), Jeffrey L. Rotman/ Peter Arnold, Inc.;

30(br), Dr. E.R. Degginger; 30(bl), Keith Philpott/Image Bank; 31(br), Nigel Cattlin/Holt Studios International/Photo Researchers, Inc.; 32(bl), Randy Morse/Tom Stack & Associates; 32(cl), Biophoto Associates/ Science Source/Photo Researchers, Inc.; 32(tl), Lee Foster/FPG Int'l; 34(tl), Visuals Unlimited/T. E. Adams; 34(b), CNRI/Science Photo Library/Photo Researchers, Inc.; 35(b), Visuals Unlimited/R. Calentine; 35(c), Visuals Unlimited/A. M. Siegelman; 36(cl), SuperStock; 36(cr), Dr. E.R. Degginger, FPSA; 36(c), Stephen Frink/Corbis; 36(tr), Holt Studios Int./Photo Researchers, Inc.; 37 Visuals Unlimited/David M. Phillips; 38 David Fleetham/FPG Int'l; 39(br), Daniel Schaefer/HRW Photo; 39(tr), Milton Rand/Tom Stack & Associates; 40(tl), Mary Beth Angelo/Photo Researchers, Inc.; 41(tr), SuperStock; 41(cl), Will Crocker/Image Bank; 41(bl), Sergio Purcell/FOCA; 42(tl), CNRI/ Science Photo Library/Photo Researchers, Inc.; 42(cl), Visuals Unlimited/A. Kerstitch; 42(bl), Dr. E.R. Degginger, FPSA; 43 David Scharf/Peter Arnold; 44(tl), Visuals Unlimited/R. Calentine; 44(cr), SuperStock; 44(bc), Uniphoto; 44(cl), Stephen Dalton/NHPA; 44(br), Gail Shumway/FPG Int'l; 45(cr), Joe McDonald; 47(cl), Darryl Torckler/Stone; 47(blb), Visuals Unlimited/Cabisco; 47(blt), Paul McCormick/Image Bank; 47(tr), Robert Dunne/Photo Researchers, Inc.; 47(cr), Chesher/Photo Researchers, Inc.; 49(cr), Visuals Unlimited/Marty Snyderman; 49(tr), Andrew J. Martinez/Photo Researchers, Inc.; 49(bl), Visuals Unlimited/Daniel W. Gotshall; 51 Victoria Smith/HRW Photo; 52 Keith Philpott/Image Bank; 53(cl), Uniphoto; 53(tc), SuperStock; 54 Ken Philpott/Image Bank; 56(c), Visuals Unlimited/ Diane R. Nelson; 57(br), Mark Norman/Archfull

Chapter Three: p. 58-59 J. Schauer/Max Planck Institute; 59 Visuals Unlimited; 59 HRW Photo; 60(c), Louis Psihoyos/Matrix; 60(bc), Norbert Wu/Peter Arnold; 60(bl), Randy Morse/Tom Stack; 61 Grant Heilman; 62 Uniphoto; 63(bl), Doug Perrine/DRK Photo; 63(br), Brian Parker/Tom Stack; 63(cl), Animals Animals; 63(bc), Visuals Unlimited/Ken Lucas; 63(c), Bruce Coleman; 65(tr), Hans Reinhard/Bruce Coleman; 65(c), Index Stock; 65(b), Martin Barraud/Stone; 66(tl), Visuals Unlimited/Science Visuals Unlimited; 66(cl), Navaswan/FPG Int'l; 67(tr), Bruce Coleman; 67(cl), Steinhart Aquarium/Tom McHugh/Photo Researchers, Inc.; 68(cl), Michael Fogden/DRK Photo; 68(bl), Visuals Unlimited/Nathan W. Cohen; 69(tr), David M. Dennis/Tom Stack & Associates; 69(br), C.K. Lorenz/Photo Researchers, Inc.; 70 Michael and Patricia Fogden; 71(tr), M.P.L. Fogden/ Bruce Coleman; 71(br), Zig Leszczynski/Animals Animals; 71(cr), Stephen Dalotn/NHPA; 72(tl), Leonard Lee Rue/Photo Researchers, Inc.; 72(tr), Breck P. Kent; 72(cl), Telegraph Color Library/FPG Int'l; 73 Visuals Unlimited/ Rob & Ann Simpson; 74(tc), Gail Shumway/FPG Int'l; 74(tl), Gail Shumway/FPG Int'l; 74(bc), Stanley Breeden/DRK Photo; 74(br), Visuals Unlimited/Joe McDonald; 76(tl), Bruce Coleman; 76(c), Mike Severns/ Stone; 76(bl), Kevin Schafer/Peter Arnold; 76(br), Wayne Lynch/DRK Photo; 77(t), Wolfgang Kaehler; 77(cr), Michael Fogden/DRK Photo; 80 Uniphoto; 81(cl), Michael Fogden/DRK Photos; 81(tr), Brian Parker/Tom Stack & Assoc.; 82 Steven David Miller/Animals Animals Earth Scenes

Chapter Four: p. 86-87 Nigle J. Dennis/Photo Researchers, Inc.; 87 HRW Photo; 88(cl), Anthony Mercieca/Photo Researchers, Inc.; 88(tr), Stan Osolinski/FPG Int'l; 88(c), Gail Shumway/FPG Int'l; 88(b - inset), Runk/Schoenberger/ Grant Heilman; 88(bl), Douglas Faulkner/Photo Researchers, Inc.; 92(b), Ben Osborne/Stone; 93(b), D. Cavagnaro/DRK Photo; 93(tr), Frans Lanting/Minden Pictures; 93(cr), Joe McDonald/DRK Photo; 94(tr), Thomas McAvoy/Time Life Syndication; 94(br), Hal H. Harrison/Grant Heilman; 95(bc), Gavriel Jecan/ Stone; 95(cr), APL/J. Carnemolla/Westlight; 95(bl), Kevin Schafer/Stone; 96(cl), Tui De Roy/Minden Pictures; 96(cr), Wayne Lankinen/Bruce Coleman; 96(tr), S. Nielsen/DRK Photo; 96(bl), Greg Vaughn/Stone; 96(br), Fritz Polking/Bruce Coleman; 97(tl), Stephen J. Krasemann/DRK Photo; 97(cr), Visuals Unlimited/S. Maslowski; 97(tr), Frans Lanting/Minden Pictures; 98(cl), Gerard Lacz/Animals Animals; 98(cr), Tim Davis/Photo Researchers, Inc.; 98(c), Nigel Dennis/Photo Researchers, Inc.; 99(cl), Hans Reinhard/Bruce Coleman; 100(tl), David E. Myers/Stone; 100(tr), Tom Tietz/Stone; 100(bl), Konrad Wothe/WestLight; 101 Kathy Bushue/Stone; 102(cl), Edwin & Peggy Bauer/ Bruce Coleman; 102(bl), Dave Watts/Tom Stack; 103(tr), Jean-Paul Ferrero/AUSCAPE; 103(cl), Hans Reinhard/Bruce Coleman; 103(bc), Art Wolfe/Stone; 104(bl), Wayne Lynch/DRK Photo; 104(cl), Visuals Unlimited/ John D. Cunningham; 105(tr), Gail Shumway/FPG Int'l; 105(tl), D. R. Kuhn/Bruce Coleman; 105(br), Lynda Richardson/Peter Arnold; 105(bl), Frans Lanting/ Minden Pictures; 106(tr), David Cavagnaro/Peter Arnold; 106(tl), John Cancalosi; 106(c), S. C. Bisserot/Bruce Coleman; 106(b), EyeWire, Inc.; 107(cr), Uniphoto; 107(tr), Gail Shumway/FPG Int'l; 107(bl), Arthur C. Smith III/Grant Heilman; 107(cl), Joe McDonald/Bruce Coleman; 108(tr), Scott Daniel Peterson/Liaison; 108(cl), Gail Shumway/FPG Int'l; 108(b), Roberto Arakaki/International Stock; 109 Art Wolfe/Stone; 110(c), Francois Gohier; 110(tr), Flip Nicklin/Minden Pictures; 110(b), Tom & Therisa Stack; 111(l), J. & P. Wegner/Animals Animals; 111(tr), Inga Spence/Tom Stack; 114(c), Frans Lanting/Minden Pictures; 115 Gerard Lacz/Animals Animals; 116 S. C. Bisserot/ Bruce Coleman; 118(b), Will & Deni McIntyre/Stone; 118(c), Tom & Pat Leeson/ Photo Researchers, Inc.; 119(br), Raymond A. Mendez/Animals Animals

Labook: "LabBook Header": "L", Corbis Images, "a", Letraset-Phototone, "b" and "B", HRW, "o" and "k", Images Copyright ©2001 PhotoDisc, Inc.; 50-51 Victoria Smith/HRW Photo; 121(cl), Michelle Bridwell/HRW Photo; 121(br), Image ©2001 PhotoDisc, Inc./HRW Photo; 122(bl), Stephanie Morris/HRW Photo; 122(cl), Victoria Smith/HRW Photo; 123(tr), Jana Birchum/HRW Photo; 128 Rod Planck/Photo Researchers, Inc.

Appendix: 142 CENCO

Sam Dudgeon/HRW Photos: all Systems of the Body background photos. p. viii-1, 18, 19, 113, 120, 121(bc), 122(br, tr), 123(tl), 127, 133(br)

Peter Van Steen/HRW Photos: p. 4(cl), 79, 99(br), 123(b), 129, 133(tr)

John Langford/HRW Photos: p. 121(tr)

Self-Check Answers

Chapter 1—Animals and Behavior

Page 6: Like other vertebrates, humans have a skull and a backbone.

Chapter 2—Invertebrates

Page 33: Because medusas swim through the water by contracting their bodies, they must have a nervous system that can control these actions. Polyps move very little, so they don't need as complex a nervous system.

Page 43: Segmented worms belong to the phylum Annelida. Centipedes are arthropods. Centipedes have jointed legs, antennae, and mandibles. Segmented worms have none of these characteristics.

Chapter 3—Fishes, Amphibians, and Reptiles

Page 69: Amphibians use their skin to absorb oxygen from the air. Their skin is thin, moist, and full of blood vessels, just like a lung.

Page 75: 1. Thick, dry skin and amniotic eggs help reptiles live on dry land. 2. The hard shell prevents fertilization, so the egg must be fertilized before the shell is added.

Chapter 4—Birds and Mammals

Page 90: 1. Down feathers are not stiff and smooth and could not give structure to the wings. They are adapted to keep the bird warm. 2. Birds need tremendous amounts of food for fuel because it takes a lot of energy to fly.

Page 104: Monotremes are mammals that lay eggs. Marsupials bear live young but carry them in pouches or skin folds before they are able to live independently. Placentals develop inside the mother's body and are nourished through a placenta before birth.

Page 109: 1. Bats bear live young, have fur, and do not have feathers. 2. Rodents and lagomorphs both are small mammals with long sensitive whiskers and gnawing teeth. Unlike rodents, lagomorphs have two sets of incisors and a short tail.